THE PLOUGH AND THE STARS

MACMILLAN AND CO., Limited
LONDON · BOMBAY · CALCUTTA · MADRAS
MELBOURNE

THE MACMILLAN COMPANY
NEW YORK · BOSTON · CHICAGO
DALLAS · SAN FRANCISCO

THE MACMILLAN CO. OF CANADA, Ltd.
TORONTO

Sean O'Casey

THE PLOUGH AND THE STARS

A TRAGEDY IN FOUR ACTS

BY

SEAN O'CASEY

WITH A PORTRAIT

MACMILLAN AND CO., LIMITED
ST. MARTIN'S STREET, LONDON
1926

TO THE GAY LAUGH OF MY MOTHER
AT THE GATE OF THE GRAVE

The Plough and the Stars was first produced in the Abbey Theatre, Dublin, on Monday, February 8, 1926, with the following cast :

COMMANDANT JACK CLITHEROE . .	F. J. McCormick
NORA CLITHEROE	Shelah Richards
PETER FLYNN	Eric Gorman
THE YOUNG COVEY	Michael J. Dolan
FLUTHER GOOD.	Barry Fitzgerald
BESSIE BURGESS	Maureen Delany
MRS. GOGAN	May Craig
MOLLSER	Kitty Curling
CAPTAIN BRENNAN	Gabriel J. Fallon
LIEUT. LANGON	Arthur Shields
ROSIE REDMOND	Ria Mooney
A BARMAN	P. J. Carolan
A WOMAN	Eileen Crowe
THE VOICE	J. Stephenson
CORPORAL STODDART	P. J. Carolan
SERGEANT TINLEY	J. Stephenson

The Play was produced by Lennox Robinson.

THE CHARACTERS IN THE PLAY

JACK CLITHEROE (*a bricklayer*), *Commandant in the Irish Citizen Army*

NORA CLITHEROE, *his wife*

PETER FLYNN (*a labourer*), *Nora's uncle*   *Residents*

THE YOUNG COVEY (*a fitter*), *Clitheroe's cousin*   *in the*

BESSIE BURGESS (*a street fruit-vendor*)   *Tenement.*

MRS. GOGAN (*a charwoman*)

MOLLSER, *her consumptive child*

FLUTHER GOOD (*a carpenter*)

LIEUT. LANGON (*a Civil Servant*), *of the Irish Volunteers.*

CAPT. BRENNAN (*a chicken butcher*), *of the Irish Citizen Army.*

CORPORAL STODDART, *of the Wiltshires.*

SERGEANT TINLEY, *of the Wiltshires.*

ROSIE REDMOND, *a daughter of "the Digs."*

A BAR-TENDER.

A WOMAN.

THE FIGURE IN THE WINDOW.

ACT I.—The living-room of the Clitheroe flat in a Dublin tenement.

ACT II.—A public-house, outside of which a meeting is being held.

ACT III.—The street outside the Clitheroe tenement.

ACT IV.—The room of Bessie Burgess.

TIME.—Acts I. and II., November 1915 ; Acts III. and IV., Easter Week, 1916. A few days elapse between Acts III. and IV.

viii

ACT I

SCENE: *The home of the* CLITHEROES. *It consists of the front and back drawing-rooms in a fine old Georgian house, struggling for its life against the assaults of time, and the more savage assaults of the tenants. The room shown is the back drawing-room, wide, spacious and lofty. At back is the entrance to the front drawing-room. The space, originally occupied by folding doors, is now draped with casement cloth of a dark purple, decorated with a design in reddish-purple and cream. One of the curtains is pulled aside, giving a glimpse of front drawing-room, at the end of which can be seen the wide, lofty windows looking out into the street. The room directly in front of the audience is furnished in a way that suggests an attempt towards a finer expression of domestic life. The large fireplace on right is of wood, painted to look like marble (the original has been taken away by the landlord).*

On the mantelshelf are two candlesticks of dark carved wood.   Between them is a small clock.   Over the clock is hanging a calendar which displays a picture of "The Sleeping Venus."   In the centre of the breast of the chimney hangs a picture of Robert Emmett. On the right of the entrance to the front drawing-room is a copy of "The Gleaners," on the opposite side a copy of "The Angelus." Underneath "The Gleaners" is a chest of drawers on which stands a green bowl filled with scarlet dahlias and white chrysanthemums.   Near to the fireplace is a settee which at night forms a double bed for CLITHEROE *and* NORA. *Underneath "The Angelus" are a number of shelves containing saucepans and a frying-pan.   Under these is a table on which are various articles of delph ware. Near the end of the room opposite to the fireplace is a gate-legged table, covered with a cloth.   On top of the table a huge cavalry sword is lying.   To the right is a door which leads to a lobby from which the staircase leads to the hall.   The floor is covered with a dark green linoleum.   The room is dim except where it is illuminated from the glow of the fire.   Through the window of the room at back can be seen the flaring of the flame of a*

2

gasolene lamp giving light to workmen repairing the street.   Occasionally can be heard the clang of crowbars striking the sets.   FLUTHER GOOD *is repairing the lock of door, Right.   A claw hammer is on a chair beside him, and he has a screw-driver in his hand.   He is a man of forty years of age, rarely surrendering to thoughts of anxiety, fond of his "oil" but determined to conquer the habit before he dies. He is square-jawed and harshly featured; under the left eye is a scar, and his nose is bent from a smashing blow received in a fistic battle long ago.   He is bald, save for a few peeping tufts of reddish hair around his ears; and his upper lip is hidden by a scrubby red moustache, embroidered here and there with a grey hair.   He is dressed in a seedy black suit, cotton shirt with a soft collar, and wears a very respectable little black bow.   On his head is a faded jerry hat, which, when he is excited, he has a habit of knocking farther back on his head, in a series of taps.   In an argument he usually fills with sound and fury generally signifying a row.   He is in his shirt sleeves at present, and wears a soiled white apron, from a pocket in which sticks a carpenter's two-foot rule.   He has just finished the job of putting on a new lock, and,*

3

filled with satisfaction, he is opening and shutting the door, enjoying the completion of a work well done. Sitting at the fire, airing a white shirt, is PETER FLYNN. *He is a little, thin bit of a man, with a face shaped like a lozenge; on his cheeks and under his chin is a straggling wiry beard of a dirty-white and lemon hue. His face invariably wears a look of animated anguish, mixed with irritated defiance, as if everybody was at war with him, and he at war with everybody. He is cocking his head in such a way that suggests resentment at the presence of* FLUTHER, *who pays no attention to him, apparently, but is really furtively watching him. Peter is clad in a singlet, white whipcord knee-breeches, and is in his stocking feet.*

A voice is heard speaking outside of door, Left (it is that of MRS. GOGAN).

MRS. GOGAN (*outside*). Who are you lookin' for, sir? Who? Mrs. Clitheroe? . . . Oh, excuse me. Oh ay, up this way. She's out, I think: I seen her goin'. Oh, you've somethin' for her; oh, excuse me. You're from Arnott's. . . . I see. . . . You've a parcel for her. . . . Righto. . . . I'll take it. . . . I'll give it to her the minute she comes in. . . .

4

It'll be quite safe. . . . Oh, sign that. . . .
Excuse me. . . . Where? . . . Here? . . .
No, there; righto. Am I to put Maggie
or Mrs.? What is it? You dunno? Oh,
excuse me.

> (MRS. GOGAN *opens the door and comes in.*
> *She is a doleful looking little woman of*
> *forty, insinuating manner and sallow*
> *complexion.   She is fidgety and nervous,*
> *terribly talkative, has a habit of taking*
> *up things that may be near her and*
> *fiddling with them while she is speaking.*
> *Her heart is aflame with curiosity, and*
> *a fly could not come into nor go out of the*
> *house without her knowing.   She has a*
> *draper's parcel in her hand, the knot of*
> *the twine tying it is untied.* PETER,
> *more resentful of this intrusion than of*
> FLUTHER'S *presence, gets up from the*
> *chair, and without looking around, his*
> *head carried at an angry cock, marches*
> *into the room at back.*

MRS. GOGAN (*removing the paper and opening*
the cardboard box it contains). I wondher what's
this now? A hat! (*She takes out a hat, black,*
with decorations in red and gold.) God, she's
goin' to th' divil lately for style! That hat,
now, cost more than a penny. Such notions of

5

upperosity she's gettin'. (*Putting the hat on her head*) Oh, swank, what! (*She replaces it in parcel.*)

FLUTHER. She's a pretty little Judy, all the same.

MRS. GOGAN. Ah, she is, an' she isn't. There's prettiness an' prettiness in it. I'm always sayin' that her skirts are a little too short for a married woman. An' to see her, sometimes of an evenin', in her glad-neck gown would make a body's blood run cold. I do be ashamed of me life before her husband. An' th' way she thries to be polite, with her "Good mornin', Mrs. Gogan," when she's goin' down, an' her "Good evenin', Mrs. Gogan," when she's comin' up. But there's politeness an' politeness in it.

FLUTHER. They seem to get on well together, all th' same.

MRS. GOGAN. Ah, they do, an' they don't. The pair o' them used to be like two turtle doves always billin' an' cooin'. You couldn't come into th' room but you'd feel, instinctive like, that they'd just been afther kissin' an' cuddlin' each other. . . . It often made me shiver, for, afther all, there's kissin' an' cuddlin' in it. But I'm thinkin' he's beginnin' to take things more quietly; the mysthery of havin' a woman's a

6

mysthery no longer. . . . She dhresses herself
to keep him with her, but its no use—afther
a month or two, th' wondher of a woman
wears off.

FLUTHER. I dunno, I dunno. Not wishin'
to say anything derogatory, I think it's all a
question of location: when a man finds th'
wondher of one woman beginnin' to die, it's
usually beginnin' to live in another.

MRS. GOGAN. She's always grumblin' about
havin' to live in a tenement house. " I wouldn't
like to spend me last hour in one, let alone live
me life in a tenement," says she. " Vaults,"
says she, " that are hidin' th' dead, instead of
homes that are sheltherin' th' livin'." " Many
a good one," says I, " was reared in a tenement
house." Oh, you know, she's a well-up little
lassie, too; able to make a shillin' go where
another would have to spend a pound. She's
wipin' th' eyes of th' Covey an' poor oul' Pether
—everybody knows that—screwin' every penny
she can out o' them, in ordher to turn th' place
into a babby-house. An' she has th' life
frightened out o' them; washin' their face,
combin' their hair, wipin' their feet, brushin'
their clothes, thrimmin' their nails, cleanin'
their teeth—God Almighty, you'd think th' poor
men were undhergoin' penal servitude.

7

FLUTHER (*with an exclamation of disgust*). A-a-ah, that's goin' beyond th' beyonds in a tenement house. That's a little bit too derogatory.

> (PETER *enters from room, Back, head elevated and resentful fire in his eyes; he is still in his singlet and trousers, but is now wearing a pair of unlaced boots—possibly to be decent in the presence of* MRS. GOGAN. *He places the white shirt, which he has carried in on his arm, on the back of a chair near the fire, and, going over to the chest of drawers, he opens drawer after drawer, looking for something; as he fails to find it he closes each drawer with a snap; he pulls out pieces of linen neatly folded, and bundles them back again any way.*)

PETER (*in accents of anguish*). Well, God Almighty, give me patience!

> (*He returns to room, Back, giving the shirt a vicious turn as he passes.*)

MRS. GOGAN. I wondher what is he foostherin' for now?

FLUTHER. He's adornin' himself for th' meeting to-night. (*Pulling a handbill from his pocket and reading*) "Great Demonstration an' torchlight procession around places in th' city sacred to th' memory of Irish Patriots to be

concluded be a meetin', at which will be taken
an oath of fealty to th' Irish Republic.   Formation in Parnell Square at eight o'clock."   Well,
they can hold it for Fluther.   I'm up th' pole;
no more dhrink for Fluther.   It's three days
now since I touched a dhrop, an' I feel a new
man already.

MRS. GOGAN. Isn't oul' Peter a funny lookin'
little man? . . . Like somethin' you'd pick off
a Christmas Tree. . . . When he's dhressed
up in his canonicals, you'd wondher where he'd
been got.   God forgive me, when I see him in
them, I always think he must ha' had a Mormon
for a father!   He an' th' Covey can't abide each
other; th' pair o' them is always at it, thryin'
to best each other.   There'll be blood dhrawn
one o' these days.

FLUTHER. How is it that Clitheroe himself,
now, doesn't have anythin' to do with th'
Citizen Army?   A couple o' months ago, an'
you'd hardly ever see him without his gun, an'
th' Red Hand o' Liberty Hall in his hat.

MRS. GOGAN. Just because he wasn't made a
Captain of.   He wasn't goin' to be in anything
where he couldn't be conspishuous.   He was so
cocksure o' being made one that he bought a
Sam Brown belt, an' was always puttin' it on
an' standin' at th' door showing it off, till th'

9

man came an' put out th' street lamps on him. God, I think he used to bring it to bed with him! But I'm tellin' you herself was delighted that that cock didn't crow, for she's like a clockin' hen if he leaves her sight for a minute.

(*While she is talking she takes up book after book from the table, looks into each of them in a near-sighted way, and then leaves them back. She now lifts up the sword, and proceeds to examine it.*)

MRS. GOGAN. Be th' look of it, this must ha' been a general's sword. . . . All th' gold lace an' th' fine figaries on it. . . . Sure it's twiced too big for him.

FLUTHER. A-ah; it's a baby's rattle he ought to have, an' he as he is with thoughts tossin' in his head of what may happen to him on th' day o' judgement.

(PETER *has entered, and seeing* MRS. GOGAN *with the sword, goes over to her, pulls it resentfully out of her hands, and marches into the room, Back, without speaking.*)

MRS. GOGAN (*as* PETER *whips the sword*). Oh, excuse me! . . . (*To* FLUTHER) Isn't he th' surly oul' rascal.

FLUTHER. Take no notice of him. . . . You'd think he was dumb, but when you get

10

his goat, or he has a few jars up, he's vice versa.
(*He coughs.*)

MRS. GOGAN (*she has now sidled over as far as
the shirt hanging on the chair*). Oh, you've got a
cold on you, Fluther.

FLUTHER (*carelessly*). Ah, it's only a little one.

MRS. GOGAN. You'd want to be careful, all
th' same.   I knew a woman, a big lump of
a woman, red-faced an' round-bodied, a little
awkward on her feet; you'd think, to look at
her, she could put out her two arms an' lift a
two-storied house on th' top of her head; got
a ticklin' in her throat, an' a little cough, an' th'
next mornin' she had a little catchin' in her
chest, an' they had just time to wet her lips with
a little rum, an' off she went.

(*She begins to look at and handle the shirt.*)

FLUTHER (*a little nervously*). It's only a little
cold I have; there's nothing derogatory wrong
with me.

MRS. GOGAN. I dunno; there's many a man
this minute lowerin' a pint, thinkin' of a woman,
or pickin' out a winner, or doin' work as you're
doin', while th' hearse dhrawn be th' horses
with the black plumes is dhrivin' up to his own
hall door, an' a voice that he doesn't hear is
muttherin' in his ear, " Earth to earth, an'
ashes t' ashes, an' dust to dust."

FLUTHER (*faintly*). A man in th' pink o' health should have a holy horror of allowin' thoughts o' death to be festherin' in his mind, for (*with a frightened cough*) be God, I think I'm afther gettin' a little catch in me chest that time—it's a creepy thing to be thinkin' about.

MRS. GOGAN. It is, an' it isn't; it's both bad an' good. . . . It always gives meself a kind o' thresspassin' joy to feel meself movin' along in a mournin' coach, an' me thinkin' that, maybe, th' next funeral 'll be me own, an' glad, in a quiet way, that this is somebody else's.

FLUTHER. An' a curious kind of a gaspin' for breath—I hope there's nothin' derogatory wrong with me.

MRS. GOGAN (*examining the shirt*). Frills on it, like a woman's petticoat.

FLUTHER. Suddenly gettin' hot, an' then, just as suddenly, gettin' cold.

MRS. GOGAN (*holding out the shirt towards* FLUTHER). How would you like to be wearin' this Lord Mayor's nightdhress, Fluther?

FLUTHER (*vehemently*). Blast you an' your nightshirt! Is a man fermentin' with fear to stick th' showin' off to him of a thing that looks like a shinin' shroud?

MRS. GOGAN. Oh, excuse me!

(PETER *has again entered, and he pulls the*

shirt from the hands of MRS. GOGAN,
*replacing it on the chair.   He returns
to room.*)

PETER (*as he goes out*). Well, God Almighty,
give me patience!

MRS. GOGAN (*to* PETER). Oh, excuse me!

(*There is heard a cheer from the men work-
ing outside on the street, followed by the
clang of tools being thrown down, then
silence.   The glare of the gasolene light
diminishes and finally goes out.*)

MRS. GOGAN (*running into the back room to look
out of the window*). What's the men repairin'
th' streets cheerin' for?

FLUTHER (*sitting down weakly on a chair*).
You can't sneeze but that oul' one wants to
know th' why an' th' wherefore. . . . I feel as
dizzy as bedamned!   I hope I didn't give up
th' beer too suddenly.

(*The* COVEY *comes in by door, Right.   He
is about twenty-five, tall, thin, with lines
on his face that form a perpetual protest
against life as he conceives it to be.
Heavy seams fall from each side of nose,
down around his lips, as if they were
suspenders keeping his mouth from falling.   He speaks in a slow, wailing
drawl; more rapidly when he is excited.*

13

*He is dressed in dungarees, and is wear-
ing a vividly red tie. He flings his
cap with a gesture of disgust on
the table, and begins to take off his
overalls.*)

MRS. GOGAN (*to the* COVEY, *as she runs back
into the room*). What's after happenin', Covey?

THE COVEY (*with contempt*). Th' job's stopped.
They've been mobilized to march in th' demonstration to-night undher th' Plough an' th' Stars.
Didn't you hear them cheerin', th' mugs. They
have to renew their political baptismal vows to
be faithful in seculo seculorum.

FLUTHER (*forgetting his fear in his indignation*).
There's no reason to bring religion into it.   I
think we ought to have as great a regard for
religion as we can, so as to keep it out of as
many things as possible.

THE COVEY (*pausing in the taking off of his
dungarees*). Oh, you're one o' the boys that
climb into religion as high as a short Mass on
Sunday mornin's?   I suppose you'll be singin'
songs o' Sion an' songs o' Tara at th' meetin',
too.

FLUTHER. We're all Irishmen, anyhow;
aren't we?

THE COVEY (*with hand outstretched, and in a
professorial tone*). Look here, comrade, there's

14

no such thing as an Irishman, or an English-
man, or a German or a Turk; we're all only
human bein's.   Scientifically speakin', it's all a
question of the accidental gatherin' together of
mollycewels an' atoms.

>   (PETER *comes in with a collar in his hand.*
>   *He goes over to mirror, Left, and pro-*
>   *ceeds to try to put it on.*)

FLUTHER. Mollycewels an' atoms! D'ye
think I'm goin' to listen to you thryin' to juggle
Fluther's mind with complicated cunundhrums
of mollycewels an' atoms?

THE COVEY (*rather loudly*). There's nothin'
complicated in it.   There's no fear o' th'
Church tellin' you that mollycewels is a stickin'
together of millions of atoms o' sodium, carbon,
potassium o' iodide, etcetera, that, accordin' to
th' way they're mixed, make a flower, a fish, a
star that you see shinin' in th' sky, or a man
with a big brain like me, or a man with a little
brain like you!

FLUTHER (*more loudly still*). There's no necessity to be raisin' your voice; shoutin's no mani-
festin' forth of a growin' mind.

PETER (*struggling with his collar*). God, give
me patience with this thing. . . . She makes
these collars as stiff with starch as a shinin' band
o' solid steel!   She does it purposely to thry

an' twart me.   If I can't get it on th' singlet,
how, in th' Name o' God, am I goin' to get it
on th' shirt?

THE COVEY (*loudly*).   There's no use o' arguin'
with you; it's education you want, comrade.

FLUTHER. The Covey an' God made th'
world, I suppose, wha'?

THE COVEY. When I hear some men talkin'
I'm inclined to disbelieve that th' world's eight-
hundhred million years old, for it's not long
since th' fathers o' some o' them crawled out o'
th' sheltherin' slime o' the sea.

MRS. GOGAN (*from room at back*). There,
they're afther formin' fours, an' now they're
goin' to march away.

FLUTHER (*scornfully*). Mollycewels! (*He
begins to untie his apron*) What about Adam an'
Eve?

THE COVEY. Well, what about them?

FLUTHER (*fiercely*). What about them, you?

THE COVEY. Adam an' Eve!   Is that as far
as you've got?   Are you still thinkin' there was
nobody in th' world before Adam an' Eve?
(*Loudly*) Did you ever hear, man, of th' skeleton
of th' man o' Java?

PETER (*casting the collar from him*). Blast it,
blast it, blast it!

FLUTHER (*viciously folding his apron*). Ah,

16

you're not goin' to be let tap your rubbidge o' thoughts into th' mind o' Fluther.

THE COVEY. You're afraid to listen to th' thruth!

FLUTHER. Who's afraid?

THE COVEY. You are!

FLUTHER. G'way, you wurum!

THE COVEY. Who's a worum?

FLUTHER. You are, or you wouldn't talk th' way you're talkin'.

THE COVEY. Th' oul', ignorant savage leppin' up in you, when science shows you that th' head of your god is an empty one. Well, I hope you're enjoyin' th' blessin' o' havin' to live be th' sweat of your brow.

FLUTHER. You'll be kickin' an' yellin' for th' priest yet, me boyo. I'm not goin' to stand silent an' simple listenin' to a thick like you makin' a maddenin' mockery o' God Almighty. It 'ud be a nice derogatory thing on me conscience, an' me dyin', to look back in rememberin' shame of talkin' to a word-weavin' little ignorant yahoo of a red flag Socialist!

MRS. GOGAN (*she has returned to the front room, and has wandered around looking at things in general, and is now in front of the fireplace looking at the picture hanging over it*). For God's sake, Fluther, dhrop it; there's always th' makin's of

17   C

a row in th' mention of religion. . . . (*Looking at picture*) God bless us, it's a naked woman!

FLUTHER (*coming over to look at it*). What's undher it? (*Reading*) "Georgina: The Sleepin' Vennis." Oh, that's a terrible picture; oh, that's a shockin' picture! Oh, th' one that got that taken, she must have been a prime lassie!

PETER (*who also has come over to look, laughing, with his body bent at the waist, and his head slightly tilted back*). Hee, hee, hee, hee, hee!

FLUTHER (*indignantly, to* PETER). What are you hee, hee-in' for? That's a nice thing to be hee, hee-in at. Where's your morality, man?

MRS. GOGAN. God forgive us, it's not right to be lookin' at it.

FLUTHER. It's nearly a derogatory thing to be in th' room where it is.

MRS. GOGAN (*giggling hysterically*). I couldn't stop any longer in th' same room with three men, afther lookin' at it!   (*She goes out.*)

> (*The* COVEY, *who has divested himself of his dungarees, throws them with a contemptuous motion on top of Peter's white shirt.*)

PETER (*plaintively*). Where are you throwin' them? Are you thryin' to twart an' torment me again?

THE COVEY. Who's thryin' to twart you?

PETER (*flinging the dungarees violently on the floor*). You're not goin' to make me lose me temper, me young Covey.

THE COVEY (*flinging the white shirt on the floor*). If you're Nora's pet, aself, you're not goin' to get your way in everything.

PETER (*plaintively, with his eyes looking up at the ceiling*). I'll say nothin'. . . . I'll leave you to th' day when th' all-pitiful, all-merciful, all-lovin' God'll be handin' you to th' angels to be rievin' an' roastin' you, tearin' an' tormentin' you, burnin' an' blastin' you!

THE COVEY. Aren't you th' little malignant oul' bastard, you lemon-whiskered oul' swine!

(PETER *runs to the sword, draws it, and makes for the* COVEY, *who dodges him around the table;* PETER *has no intention of striking, but the* COVEY *wants to take no chances.*)

THE COVEY (*dodging*). Fluther, hold him, there. It's a nice thing to have a lunatic like this lashin' around with a lethal weapon!

(*The* COVEY *darts out of room, Right, slamming the door in the face of* PETER.)

PETER (*battering and pulling at the door*). Lemme out, lemme out; isn't it a poor thing for a man who wouldn't say a word against his greatest enemy to have to listen to that Covey's twartin' animosities, shovin' poor, patient people into a lashin' out of curses that darken his soul with th' shadow of th' wrath of th' last day!

FLUTHER. Why d'ye take notice of him? If he seen you didn't, he'd say nothin' derogatory.

PETER. I'll make him stop his laughin' an' leerin', jibin' an' jeerin' an' scarifyin' people with his corner-boy insinuations! . . . He's always thryin' to rouse me: if it's not a song, it's a whistle; if it isn't a whistle, it's a cough. But you can taunt an' taunt—I'm laughin' at you; he, hee, hee, hee, hee, heee!

THE COVEY (*singing through the keyhole*):

Dear harp o' me counthry, in darkness I found thee,
The dark chain of silence had hung o'er thee long—

PETER (*frantically*). Jasus, d'ye hear that? D'ye hear him soundin' forth his divil-souled song o' provocation?

THE COVEY (*singing as before*):

When proudly, me own island harp, I unbound thee,
An' gave all thy chords to light, freedom an' song!

PETER (*battering at door*). When I get out I'll do for you, I'll do for you, I'll do for you!

THE COVEY (*through the keyhole*). Cuckoo-oo!

    (NORA *enters by door, Right. She is a
        young woman of twenty-two, alert, swift,
        full of nervous energy, and a little*

*anxious to get on in the world. The
firm lines of her face are considerably
opposed by a soft, amorous mouth, and
gentle eyes. When her firmness fails
her, she persuades with her feminine
charm. She is dressed in a tailor-made
costume, and wears around her neck a
silver fox fur.*)

NORA (*running in and pushing* PETER *away
from the door*). Oh, can I not turn me back but
th' two o' yous are at it like a pair o' fightin'
cocks! Uncle Peter . . . Uncle Peter . . .
UNCLE PETER!

PETER (*vociferously*). Oh, Uncle Peter, Uncle
Peter be damned! D'ye think I'm goin' to give
a free pass to th' young Covey to turn me
whole life into a Holy Manual o' penances an'
martyrdoms?

THE COVEY (*angrily rushing into the room*). If
you won't exercise some sort o' conthrol over
that Uncle Peter o' yours, there'll be a funeral,
an' it won't be me that'll be in th' hearse!

NORA (*between* PETER *and the* COVEY, *to the*
COVEY). Are yous always goin' to be tearin'
down th' little bit of respectability that a body's
thryin' to build up? Am I always goin' to be
havin' to nurse yous into th' hardy habit o'
thryin' to keep up a little bit of appearance?

THE COVEY. Why weren't you here to see th' way he run at me with th' sword?

PETER. What did you call me a lemon-whiskered oul' swine for?

NORA. If th' two o' yous don't thry to make a generous altheration in your goin's on, an' keep on thryin' t' inaugurate th' customs o' th' rest o' th' house into this place, yous can flit into other lodgin's where your bowsey battlin' 'ill meet, maybe, with an encore.

PETER (*to* NORA). Would you like to be called a lemon-whiskered oul' swine?

NORA. If you attempt to wag that sword of yours at anybody again, it'll have to be taken off you an' put in a safe place away from babies that don't know th' danger o' them things.

PETER (*at entrance to room, Back*). Well, I'm not goin' to let anybody call me a lemon-whiskered oul' swine. (*He goes in.*)

FLUTHER (*trying the door*). Openin' an' shuttin' now with a well-mannered motion, like a door of a select bar in a high-class pub.

NORA (*to the* COVEY, *as she lays table for tea*). An', once for all, Willie, you'll have to thry to deliver yourself from th' desire to practice o' provokin' oul' Pether into a wild forgetfulness of what's proper an' allowable in a respectable home.

22

THE COVEY. Well, let him mind his own business, then. Yestherday, I caught him hee-hee-in' out of him an' he readin' bits out of Jenersky's *Thesis on th' Origin, Development an' Consolidation of th' Evolutionary Idea of th' Proletariat.*

NORA. Now, let it end at that, for God's sake; Jack'll be in any minute, an' I'm not goin' to have th' quiet of his evenin' tossed about in an everlastin' uproar between you an' Uncle Pether. (*To* FLUTHER) Well, did you manage to settle th' lock, yet, Mr. Good?

FLUTHER (*opening and shutting door*). It's betther than a new one, now, Mrs. Clitheroe; it's almost ready to open and shut of its own accord.

NORA (*giving him a coin*). You're a whole man. How many pints will that get you?

FLUTHER (*seriously*). Ne'er a one at all, Mrs. Clitheroe, for Fluther's on th' wather waggon now. You could stan' where you're stannin' chantin', " Have a glass o' malt, Fluther; Fluther, have a glass o' malt," till th' bells would be ringin' th' ould year out an' th' New Year in, an' you'd have as much chance o' movin' Fluther as a tune on a tin whistle would move a deaf man an' he dead.

23

(*As* NORA *is opening and shutting door,* MRS. BESSIE BURGESS *appears at it. She is a woman of forty, vigorously built. Her face is a dogged one, hardened by toil, and a little coarsened by drink. She looks scornfully and viciously at* NORA *for a few moments before she speaks.*)

BESSIE. Puttin' a new lock on her door . . . afraid her poor neighbours ud break through an' steal. . . . (*In a loud tone*) Maybe, now, they're a damn sight more honest than your ladyship . . . checkin' th' children playin' on th' stairs . . . gettin' on th' nerves of your ladyship. . . . Complainin' about Bessie Burgess singin' her hymns at night, when she has a few up. . . . (*She comes in half-way on the threshold, and screams*) Bessie Burgess 'll sing whenever she damn well likes!

(NORA *tries to shut door, but* BESSIE *violently shoves it in, and, gripping* NORA *by the shoulders, shakes her.*)

BESSIE. You little over-dhressed throllope, you, for one pin, I'd paste th' white face o' you!

NORA (*frightened*). Fluther, Fluther!

FLUTHER (*running over and breaking the hold of* BESSIE *from* NORA). Now, now, Bessie, Bessie, leave poor Mrs. Clitheroe alone; she'd do no

one any harm, an' minds no one's business but
her own.

BESSIE. Why is she always thryin' to speak
proud things, an' lookin' like a mighty one in
th' congregation o' th' people!

(NORA *sinks frightened on to the couch as*
JACK CLITHEROE *enters. He is a tall,
well-made fellow of twenty-five. His
face has none of the strength of* NORA's.
*It is a face in which is the desire for
authority, without the power to attain it.*)

CLITHEROE (*excitedly*). What's up? what's
afther happenin'?

FLUTHER. Nothin', Jack. Nothin'. It's all
over now. Come on, Bessie, come on.

CLITHEROE (*to* NORA). What's wrong, Nora?
Did she say anything to you?

NORA. She was bargin' out of her, an' I only
told her to g'up ower o' that to her own place;
an' before I knew where I was, she flew at me
like a tiger, an' thried to guzzle me!

CLITHEROE (*going to door and speaking to*
BESSIE). Get up to your own place, Mrs.
Burgess, and don't you be interferin' with my
wife, or it'll be th' worse for you. . . . Go on,
go on!

BESSIE (*as* CLITHEROE *is pushing her out*).
Mind who you're pushin', now. . . . I attend

me place o' worship, anyhow . . . not like some o' them that go to neither church, chapel nor meetin' house. . . . If me son was home from th' threnches he'd see me righted.

(BESSIE *and* FLUTHER *depart, and* CLITHEROE *closes the door.*)

CLITHEROE (*going over to* NORA, *and putting his arm around her*). There, don't mind that old bitch, Nora, darling; I'll soon put a stop to her interferin'.

NORA. Some day or another, when I'm here be meself, she'll come in an' do somethin' desperate.

CLITHEROE (*kissing her*). Oh, sorra fear of her doin' anythin' desperate. I'll talk to her to-morrow when she's sober. A taste o' me mind that'll shock her into the sensibility of behavin' herself!

(NORA *gets up and settles the table. She sees the dungarees on the floor and stands looking at them, then she turns to the* COVEY, *who is reading Jenersky's "Thesis" at the fire.*)

NORA. Willie, is that th' place for your dungarees?

THE COVEY (*getting up and lifting them from the floor*). Ah, they won't do th' floor any harm, will they?   (*He carries them into room, Back.*)

26

NORA (*calling*). Uncle Peter, now Uncle Peter; tea's ready.

> (PETER *and the* COVEY *come in from room, Back; they all sit down to tea.* PETER *is in full dress of the Foresters: green coat, gold braided; white breeches, top boots, frilled shirt. He carries the slouch hat, with the white ostrich plume, and the sword in his hands. They eat for a few moments in silence, the* COVEY *furtively looking at* PETER *with scorn in his eyes.* PETER *knows it and is fidgety.*)

THE COVEY (*provokingly*). Another cut o' bread, Uncle Peter?

> (PETER *maintains a dignified silence.*)

CLITHEROE. It's sure to be a great meetin' to-night. We ought to go, Nora.

NORA (*decisively*). I won't go, Jack; you can go if you wish.

> (*A pause.*)

THE COVEY. D'ye want th' sugar, Uncle Peter?

PETER (*explosively*). Now, are you goin' to start your thryin' an' your twartin' again?

NORA. Now, Uncle Peter, you musn't be so touchy; Willie has only assed you if you wanted th' sugar.

PETER. He doesn't care a damn whether I

want th' sugar or no.   He's only thryin' to twart me!

NORA (*angrily, to the* COVEY). Can't you let him alone, Willie?   If he wants the sugar, let him stretch his hand out an' get it himself!

THE COVEY (*to* PETER). Now, if you want the sugar, you can stretch out your hand and get it yourself!

CLITHEROE. To-night is th' first chance that Brennan has got of showing himself off since they made a Captain of him—why, God only knows.   It'll be a treat to see him swankin' it at th' head of the Citizen Army carryin' th' flag of the Plough an' th' Stars. . . . (*Looking roguishly at* NORA) He was sweet on you, once, Nora?

NORA. He may have been. . . . I never liked him.   I always thought he was a bit of a thick.

THE COVEY. They're bringin' nice disgrace on that banner now.

CLITHEROE (*remonstratively*). How are they bringin' disgrace on it?

THE COVEY (*snappily*). Because it's a Labour flag, an' was never meant for politics. . . . What does th' design of th' field plough, bearin' on it th' stars of th' heavenly plough, mean, if it's not Communism?   It's a flag that should

28

only be used when we're buildin' th' barricades to fight for a Workers' Republic!

PETER (*with a puff of derision*). P-phuh.

THE COVEY (*angrily*). What are you phuhin' out o' you for? Your mind is th' mind of a mummy. (*Rising*) I betther go an' get a good place to have a look at Ireland's warriors passin' by.

> (*He goes into room, Left, and returns with his cap.*)

NORA (*to the* COVEY). Oh, Willie, brush your clothes before you go.

THE COVEY. Oh, they'll do well enough.

NORA. Go an' brush them; th' brush is in th' drawer there.

> (*The* COVEY *goes to the drawer, muttering, gets the brush, and starts to brush his clothes.*)

THE COVEY (*singing at* PETER, *as he does so*):

> Oh, where's th' slave so lowly,
> Condemn'd to chains unholy,
> Who, could he burst his bonds at first,
> Would pine beneath them slowly?
>
> We tread th' land that . . . bore us,
> Th' green flag glitters . . . o'er us,
> Th' friends we've tried are by our side,
> An' th' foe we hate . . . before us!

29

PETER (*leaping to his feet in a whirl of rage*). Now, I'm tellin' you, me young Covey, once for all, that I'll not stick any longer these tittherin' taunts of yours, rovin' around to sing your slights an' slandhers, reddenin' th' mind of a man to th' thinkin' an' sayin' of things that sicken his soul with sin! (*Hysterically; lifting up a cup to fling at the* COVEY) Be God, I'll——

CLITHEROE (*catching his arm*). Now then, none o' that, none o' that!

NORA. Uncle Pether, Uncle Pether, UNCLE PETHER!

THE COVEY (*at the door about to go out*). Isn't that th' malignant oul' varmint! Lookin' like th' illegitimate son of an illegitimate child of a corporal in th' Mexican army!

(*He goes out.*)

PETER (*plaintively*). He's afther leavin' me now in such a state of agitation that I won't be able to do meself justice when I'm marchin' to th' meetin'.

NORA (*jumping up*). Oh, for God's sake, here, buckle your sword on, and go to your meetin', so that we'll have at least one hour of peace!

(*She proceeds to belt on the sword.*)

CLITHEROE (*irritably*). For God's sake hurry him up ou' o' this, Nora.

30

PETER. Are yous all goin' to thry to start to twart me now?

NORA (*putting on his plumed hat*). S-s-sh. Now, your hat's on, your house is thatched; off you pop!

(*She gently pushes him from her.*)

PETER (*going and turning as he reaches the door*). Now, if that young Covey——

NORA. Go on, go on. (*He goes.*)

(CLITHEROE *sits down in the lounge, lights a cigarette, and looks thoughtfully into the fire.* NORA *takes the things from the table, placing them on the chest of drawers. There is a pause, then she swiftly comes over to him and sits beside him.*)

NORA (*softly*). A penny for them, Jack!

CLITHEROE. Me? Oh, I was thinkin' of nothing.

NORA. You were thinkin' of th' . . . meetin' . . . Jack. When we were courtin' an' I wanted you to go, you'd say, " Oh, to hell with meetin's," an' that you felt lonely in cheerin' crowds when I was absent. An' we weren't a month married when you began that you couldn't keep away from them.

CLITHEROE. Oh, that's enough about th' meetin'. It looks as if you wanted me to go th' way you're talkin'. You were always at me to give up th' Citizen Army, an' I gave it up; surely that ought to satisfy you.

NORA. Ay, you gave it up—because you got th' sulks when they didn't make a Captain of you. It wasn't for my sake, Jack.

CLITHEROE. For your sake or no, you're benefitin' by it, aren't you? I didn't forget this was your birthday, did I? (*He puts his arms around her*) And you liked your new hat; didn't you, didn't you? (*He kisses her rapidly several times.*)

NORA (*panting*). Jack, Jack; please, Jack! I thought you were tired of that sort of thing long ago.

CLITHEROE. Well, you're finding out now that I amn't tired of it yet, anyhow. Mrs. Clitheroe doesn't want to be kissed, sure she doesn't? (*He kisses her again*) Little, little red-lipped Nora!

NORA (*coquettishly removing his arm from around her*). Oh, yes, your little, little red-lipped Nora's a sweet little girl when th' fit seizes you; but your little, little red-lipped Nora has to clean your boots every mornin', all the same.

CLITHEROE (*with a movement of irritation*). Oh, well, if we're goin' to be snotty!

(*A pause.*)

32

NORA. It's lookin' like as if it was you that was goin' to be . . . snotty! Bridlin' up with bittherness, th' minute a body attempts t'open her mouth.

CLITHEROE. Is it any wondher, turnin' a tendher sayin' into a meanin' o' malice an' spite!

NORA. It's hard for a body to be always keepin' her mind bent on makin' thoughts that'll be no longer than th' length of your own satisfaction.   (*A pause.*)

NORA (*standing up*). If we're goin' to dhribble th' time away sittin' here like a pair o' cranky mummies, I'd be as well sewin' or doin' something about th' place.

> (*She looks appealingly at him for a few moments; he doesn't speak. She swiftly sits down beside him, and puts her arm around his neck.*)

NORA (*imploringly*). Ah, Jack, don't be so cross!

CLITHEROE (*doggedly*). Cross? I'm not cross; I'm not a bit cross. It was yourself started it.

NORA (*coaxingly*). I didn't mean to say anything out o' th' way. You take a body up too quickly, Jack. (*In an ordinary tone as if nothing of an angry nature had been said*) You didn't offer me me evenin' allowance yet.

(CLITHEROE *silently takes out a cigarette for her and himself and lights both.*)

NORA (*trying to make conversation*). How quiet th' house is now; they must be all out.

CLITHEROE (*rather shortly*). I suppose so.

NORA (*rising from the seat*). I'm longin' to show you me new hat, to see what you think of it. Would you like to see it?

CLITHEROE. Ah, I don't mind.

(NORA *suppresses a sharp reply, hesitates for a moment, then gets the hat, puts it on and stands before* CLITHEROE.)

NORA. Well, how does Mr. Clitheroe like me new hat?

CLITHEROE. It suits you, Nora, it does right enough.

(*He stands up, puts his hand beneath her chin, and tilts her head up. She looks at him roguishly. He bends down and kisses her.*)

NORA. Here, sit down, an' don't let me hear another cross word out of you for th' rest o' the night.

(*They sit down.*)

CLITHEROE (*with his arms around her*). Little, little, red-lipped Nora!

NORA (*with a coaxing movement of her body towards him*). Jack!

34

CLITHEROE (*tightening his arms around her*). Well?

NORA. You haven't sung me a song since our honeymoon.   Sing me one now, do . . . please, Jack!

CLITHEROE. What song?   " Since Maggie Went Away "?

NORA. Ah, no, Jack, not that; it's too sad. " When You said You Loved Me."

> (*Clearing his throat,* CLITHEROE *thinks for a moment, and then begins to sing.* NORA, *putting an arm around him, nestles her head on his breast and listens delightedly.*)

CLITHEROE (*singing verses following to the air of* " *When You and I were Young, Maggie* "):

Th' violets were scenting th' woods, Nora,
  Displaying their charm to th' bee,
When I first said I lov'd only you, Nora,
  An' you said you lov'd only me!

Th' chestnut blooms gleam'd through th' glade, Nora,
  A robin sang loud from a tree,
When I first said I lov'd only you, Nora,
  An' you said you lov'd only me!

Th' golden-rob'd daffodils shone, Nora,
  An' danc'd in th' breeze on th' lea;
When I first said I lov'd only you, Nora,
  An' you said you lov'd only me!

Th' trees, birds an' bees sang a song, Nora,
  Of happier transports to be,
When I first said I lov'd only you, Nora,
  An' you said you lov'd only me!

(NORA *kisses him.*)

(*A knock is heard at the door, Right; a
pause as they listen.* NORA *clings closely
to* CLITHEROE. *Another knock, more
imperative than the first.*)

CLITHEROE. I wonder who can that be,
now?

NORA (*a little nervous*). Take no notice of it,
Jack; they'll go away in a minute.

(*Another knock, followed by a voice.*)

VOICE. Commandant Clitheroe, Commandant Clitheroe, are you there? A message from
General Jim Connolly.

CLITHEROE. Damn it, it's Captain Brennan.

NORA (*anxiously*). Don't mind him, don't
mind, Jack. Don't break our happiness. . . .
Pretend we're not in. . . . Let us forget everything to-night but our two selves!

CLITHEROE (*reassuringly*). Don't be alarmed,
darling; I'll just see what he wants, an' send
him about his business.

NORA (*tremulously*). No, no. Please, Jack;
don't open it. Please, for your own little
Nora's sake!

36

CLITHEROE (*rising to open the door*). Now don't be silly, Nora.

> (CLITHEROE *opens door, and admits a young man in the full uniform of the Irish Citizen Army—green suit; slouch green hat caught up at one side by a small Red Hand badge; Sam Brown belt, with a revolver in the holster. He carries a letter in his hand. When he comes in he smartly salutes* CLITHEROE. *The young man is* CAPTAIN BRENNAN.)

CAPT. BRENNAN (*giving the letter to* CLITHEROE). A dispatch from General Connolly.

CLITHEROE (*reading. While he is doing so,* BRENNAN'S *eyes are fixed on* NORA, *who droops as she sits on the lounge*). " Commandant Clitheroe is to take command of the eighth battalion of the I.C.A. which will assemble to proceed to the meeting at nine o'clock. He is to see that all units are provided with full equipment: two days' rations and fifty rounds of ammunition. At two o'clock A.M. the army will leave Liberty Hall for a reconnaissance attack on Dublin Castle.—Com.-Gen. Connolly."

CLITHEROE. I don't understand this. Why does General Connolly call me Commandant?

CAPT. BRENNAN. Th' Staff appointed you

Commandant, and th' General agreed with their selection.

CLITHEROE. When did this happen?

CAPT. BRENNAN. A fortnight ago.

CLITHEROE. How is it word was never sent to me?

CAPT. BRENNAN. Word was sent to you. . . . I meself brought it.

CLITHEROE. Who did you give it to, then?

CAPT. BRENNAN (*after a pause*). I think I gave it to Mrs. Clitheroe, there.

CLITHEROE. Nora, d'ye hear that?

(NORA *makes no answer.*)

CLITHEROE (*there is a note of hardness in his voice*). Nora . . . Captain Brennan says he brought a letter to me from General Connolly, and that he gave it to you. . . . Where is it? What did you do with it?

NORA (*running over to him, and pleadingly putting her arms around him*). Jack, please Jack, don't go out to - night an' I'll tell you; I'll explain everything. . . . Send him away, an' stay with your own little red-lipp'd Nora.

CLITHEROE (*removing her arms from around him*). None o' this nonsense, now; I want to know what you did with th' letter?

(NORA *goes slowly to the lounge and sits down.*)

38

CLITHEROE (*angrily*). Why didn't you give me th' letter? What did you do with it? . . . (*He shakes her by the shoulder*) What did you do with th' letter?

NORA (*flaming up*). I burned it, I burned it! That's what I did with it! Is General Connolly an' th' Citizen Army goin' to be your only care? Is your home goin' to be only a place to rest in? Am I goin' to be only somethin' to provide merry-makin' at night for you? Your vanity 'll be th' ruin of you an' me yet. . . . That's what's movin' you: because they've made an officer of you, you'll make a glorious cause of what you're doin', while your little red-lipp'd Nora can go on sittin' here, makin' a companion of th' loneliness of th' night!

CLITHEROE (*fiercely*). You burned it, did you? (*He grips her arm*) Well, me good lady——

NORA. Let go—you're hurtin' me!

CLITHEROE. You deserve to be hurt. . . . Any letther that comes to me for th' future, take care that I get it. . . . D'ye hear—take care that I get it!

> (*He goes to the chest of drawers and takes out a Sam Brown belt, which he puts on, and then puts a revolver in the holster. He puts on his hat, and looks towards* NORA.)

39

CLITHEROE (*at door, about to go out*). You needn't wait up for me; if I'm in at all, it won't be before six in th' morning.

NORA (*bitterly*). I don't care if you never came back!

CLITHEROE (*to* CAPT. BRENNAN). Come along, Ned.

> (*They go out; there is a pause.* NORA *pulls the new hat from her head and with a bitter movement flings it to the other end of the room.   There is a gentle knock at door, Right, which opens, and* MOLLSER *comes into the room.   She is about fifteen, but looks to be only about ten, for the ravages of consumption have shrivelled her up.   She is pitifully worn, walks feebly, and frequently coughs. She goes over to* NORA.)

MOLLSER (*to* NORA). Mother's gone to th' meetin', an' I was feelin' terrible lonely, so I come down to see if you'd let me sit with you, thinkin' you mightn't be goin' yourself. . . . I do be terrible afraid I'll die sometime when I'm be meself. . . . I often envy you, Mrs. Clitheroe, seein' th' health you have, an' th' lovely place you have here, an' wondherin' if I'll ever be sthrong enough to be keepin' a home together for a man.   Oh, this must be some more o' the Dublin Fusiliers flyin' off to the front.

> (*Just before* MOLLSER *ceases to speak, there is heard in the distance the music of a brass band playing a regiment to the boat on the way to the front. The tune that is being played is "It's a Long Way to Tipperary"; as the band comes to the chorus, the regiment is swinging into the street by* NORA'S *house, and the voices of the soldiers can be heard lustily singing the chorus of the song.*)

It's a long way to Tipperary, it's a long way to go;
It's a long way to Tipperary, to th' sweetest girl I
    know!
Goodbye Piccadilly, farewell Leicester Square.
It's a long way to Tipperary, but my heart's right
    there!

> (NORA *and* MOLLSER *remain silently listening. As the chorus ends, and the music is faint in the distance again,* BESSIE BURGESS *appears at door, Right, which* MOLLSER *has left open.*)

BESSIE (*speaking in towards the room*). There's th' men marchin' out into th' dhread dimness o' danger, while th' lice is crawlin' about feedin' on th' fatness o' the land! But yous'll not escape from th' arrow that flieth be night, or th' sickness that wasteth be day. . . . An' ladyship an' all, as some o' them may be, they'll be scatthered abroad, like th' dust in th' darkness!

> (BESSIE *goes away;* NORA *steals over and quietly shuts the door. She comes back to the lounge and wearily throws herself on it beside* MOLLSER.)

MOLLSER (*after a pause and a cough*). Is there anybody goin', Mrs. Clitheroe, with a titther o' sense?

CURTAIN

ACT II

SCENE: *A commodious public-house at the corner of the street in which the meeting is being addressed from Platform No. 1. It is the south corner of the public-house that is visible to the audience. The counter, beginning at Back about one-fourth of the width of the space shown, comes across two-thirds of the length of the stage, and, taking a circular sweep, passes out of sight to Left. On the counter are beer-pulls, glasses and a carafe. The other three-fourths of the Back is occupied by a tall, wide, two-paned window. Beside this window at the Right is a small, box-like, panelled snug. Next to the snug is a double swing door, the entrance to that particular end of the house. Farther on is a shelf on which customers may rest their drinks. Underneath the window is a cushioned seat. Behind the counter at Back can be seen the shelves running the whole length of the*

43

counter. On these shelves can be seen the end (or the beginning) of rows of bottles. The BARMAN *is seen wiping the part of the counter which is in view.* ROSIE *is standing at the counter toying with what remains of a half of whisky in a wine-glass. She is a sturdy, well-shaped girl of twenty; pretty and pert in manner. She is wearing a cream blouse, with an obviously suggestive glad neck; a grey tweed dress, brown stockings and shoes. The blouse and most of the dress are hidden by a black shawl. She has no hat, and in her hair is jauntily set a cheap, glittering, jewelled ornament. It is an hour later.*

BARMAN (*wiping counter*). Nothin' much doin' in your line to-night, Rosie?

ROSIE. Curse o' God on th' haporth, hardly, Tom. There isn't much notice taken of a pretty petticoat of a night like this. . . . They're all in a holy mood. Th' solemn-lookin' dials on th' whole o' them an' they marchin' to th' meetin'. You'd think they were th' glorious company of th' saints, an' th' noble army of martyrs thrampin' through th' sthreets of paradise. They're all thinkin' of higher things than a girl's garthers. . . . It's a tremendous meetin'; four platforms they have

44

—there's one o' them just outside opposite th' window.

BARMAN. Oh, ay; sure when th' speaker comes (*motioning with his hand*) to th' near end, here, you can see him plain, an' hear nearly everythin' he's spoutin' out of him.

ROSIE. It's no joke thryin' to make up fifty-five shillin's a week for your keep an' laundhry, an' then taxin' you a quid for your own room if you bring home a friend for th' night. . . . If I could only put by a couple of quid for a swankier outfit, everythin' in th' garden ud look lovely——

BARMAN. Whisht, till we hear what he's sayin'.

> (*Through the window is silhouetted the figure of a tall man who is speaking to the crowd. The* BARMAN *and* ROSIE *look out of the window and listen.*)

THE VOICE OF THE MAN. It is a glorious thing to see arms in the hands of Irishmen. We must accustom ourselves to the thought of arms, we must accustom ourselves to the sight of arms, we must accustom ourselves to the use of arms. . . . Bloodshed is a cleansing and sanctifying thing, and the nation that regards it as the final horror has lost its manhood. . . . There are many things more

45

horrible than bloodshed, and slavery is one of them!

(*The figure moves away towards the Right, and is lost to sight and hearing.*)

ROSIE. It's th' sacred thruth, mind you, what that man's afther sayin'.

BARMAN. If I was only a little younger, I'd be plungin' mad into th' middle of it!

ROSIE (*who is still looking out of the window*). Oh, here's th' two gems runnin' over again for their oil!

(PETER *and* FLUTHER *enter tumultuously. They are hot, and full and hasty with the things they have seen and heard. Emotion is bubbling up in them, so that when they drink, and when they speak, they drink and speak with the fullness of emotional passion.* PETER *leads the way to the counter.*)

PETER (*splutteringly to* BARMAN). Two halves . . . (*To* FLUTHER) A meetin' like this always makes me feel as if I could dhrink Loch Erinn dhry!

FLUTHER. You couldn't feel anyway else at a time like this when th' spirit of a man is pulsin' to be out fightin' for th' thruth with his feet thremblin' on th' way, maybe to th' gallows, an' his ears tinglin' with th' faint,

46

far-away sound of burstin' rifle-shots that'll
maybe whip th' last little shock o' life out of
him that's left lingerin' in his body!

PETER. I felt a burnin' lump in me throat
when I heard th' band playin' " The Soldiers'
Song," rememberin' last hearin' it marchin' in
military formation, with th' people starin' on
both sides at us, carryin' with us th' pride an'
resolution o' Dublin to th' grave of Wolfe
Tone.

FLUTHER. Get th' Dublin men goin' an'
they'll go on full force for anything that's
thryin' to bar them away from what they're
wantin', where th' slim thinkin' counthry boyo
ud limp away from th' first faintest touch of
compromization!

PETER (*hurriedly to the* BARMAN). Two more,
Tom! . . . (*To* FLUTHER) Th' memory of
all th' things that was done, an' all th'
things that was suffered be th' people, was
boomin' in me brain. . . . Every nerve
in me body was quiverin' to do somethin'
desperate!

FLUTHER. Jammed as I was in th' crowd,
I listened to th' speeches pattherin' on th'
people's head, like rain fallin' on th' corn;
every derogatory thought went out o' me mind,
an' I said to meself, " You can die now, Fluther,

47

for you've seen th' shadow-dhreams of th' past leppin' to life in th' bodies of livin' men that show, if we were without a titther o' courage for centuries, we're vice versa now!" Looka here. (*He stretches out his arm under* PETER'S *face and rolls up his sleeve.*) The blood was BOILIN' in me veins!

> (*The silhouette of the tall figure again moves into the frame of the window speaking to the people.*)

PETER (*unaware, in his enthusiasm, of the speaker's appearance, to* FLUTHER). I was burnin' to dhraw me sword, an' wave it over me——

FLUTHER (*overwhelming* PETER). Will you stop your blatherin' for a minute, man, an' let us hear what he's sayin'!

VOICE OF THE MAN. Comrade soldiers of the Irish Volunteers and of the Citizen Army, we rejoice in this terrible war. The old heart of the earth needed to be warmed with the red wine of the battlefields. . . . Such august homage was never offered to God as this: the homage of millions of lives given gladly for love of country. And we must be ready to pour out the same red wine in the same glorious sacrifice, for without shedding of blood there is no redemption!

> (*The figure moves out of sight and hearing.*)

48

FLUTHER (*gulping down the drink that remains in his glass, and rushing out*). Come on, man; this is too good to be missed!

> (PETER *finishes his drink less rapidly, and as he is going out wiping his mouth with the back of his hand he runs into the* COVEY *coming in. He immediately erects his body like a young cock, and with his chin thrust forward, and a look of venomous dignity on his face, he marches out.*)

THE COVEY (*at counter*). Give us a glass o' malt, for God's sake, till I stimulate meself from th' shock o' seein' th' sight that's afther goin' out!

ROSIE (*all business, coming over to the counter, and standing near the* COVEY). Another one for me, Tommy; (*to the* BARMAN) th' young gentleman's ordherin' it in th' corner of his eye.

> (*The* BARMAN *brings the drink for the* COVEY, *and leaves it on the counter.* ROSIE *whips it up.*)

BARMAN. Ay, houl' on there, houl' on there, Rosie!

ROSIE (*to the* BARMAN). What are you houldin' on out o' you for? Didn't you hear th' young gentleman say that he couldn't refuse anything to a nice little bird. (*To the* COVEY)

Isn't that right, Jiggs? (*The* COVEY *says nothing*.) Didn't I know, Tommy, it would be all right? It takes Rosie to size a young man up, an' tell th' thoughts that are thremblin' in his mind. Isn't that right, Jiggs?

> (*The* COVEY *stirs uneasily, moves a little farther away, and pulls his cap over his eyes*.)

ROSIE (*moving after him*). Great meetin' that's gettin' held outside. Well, it's up to us all, anyway, to fight for our freedom.

THE COVEY (*to* BARMAN). Two more, please. (*To* ROSIE) Freedom! What's th' use o' freedom, if it's not economic freedom?

ROSIE (*emphasizing with extended arm and moving finger*). I used them very words just before you come in. "A lot o' thricksters," says I, "that wouldn't know what freedom was if they got it from their mother." . . . (*To* BARMAN) Didn't I, Tommy?

BARMAN. I disremember.

ROSIE. No, you don't disremember. Remember you said, yourself, it was all " only a flash in th' pan." Well, " flash in th' pan, or no flash in th' pan," says I, " they're not goin' to get Rosie Redmond," says I, " to fight for freedom that wouldn't be worth winnin' in a raffle! "

THE COVEY. There's only one freedom for th' workin' man: conthrol o' th' means o' production, rates of exchange an' th' means of disthribution. (*Tapping* ROSIE *on the shoulder*.) Look here, comrade, I'll leave here to-morrow night for you a copy of Jenersky's *Thesis on the Origin, Development an' Consolidation of the Evolutionary Idea of th' Proletariat.*

ROSIE (*throwing off her shawl on to the counter, and showing an exemplified glad neck, which reveals a good deal of a white bosom*). If y'ass Rosie, it's heartbreakin' to see a young fella thinkin' of anything, or admirin' anything, but silk thransparent stockin's showin' off the shape of a little lassie's legs!

(THE COVEY, *frightened, moves a little away*.)

ROSIE (*following him*). Out in th' park in th' shade of a warm summery evenin', with your little darlin' bridie to be, kissin' an' cuddlin' (*she tries to put her arm around his neck*), kissin' an' cuddlin', ay?

THE COVEY (*frightened*). Ay, what are you doin'? None o' that, now; none o' that. I've something else to do besides shinannickin' afther Judies!

(*He turns away, but* ROSIE *follows, keeping face to face with him*.)

51

ROSIE. Oh, little duckey, oh, shy little duckey! Never held a mot's hand, an' wouldn't know how to tittle a little Judy! (*She clips him under the chin.*) Tittle him undher th' chin, tittle him undher th' chin!

THE COVEY (*breaking away and running out*). Ay, go on, now; I don't want to have any meddlin' with a lassie like you!

ROSIE (*enraged*). Jasus, it's in a monasthery some of us ought to be, spendin' our holidays kneelin' on our adorers, tellin' our beads an' knockin' hell out of our buzzums!

THE COVEY (*outside*). Cuckoo-oo!

> (PETER *and* FLUTHER *come in again, followed by* MRS. GOGAN, *carrying a baby in her arms. They go over to the counter.*)

PETER (*with plaintive anger*). It's terrible that young Covey can't let me pass without proddin' at me! Did you hear him murmurin' " cuckoo " when he were passin'?

FLUTHER (*irritably*). I wouldn't be everlastin' cockin' me ear to hear every little whisper that was floatin' around about me! It's my rule never to lose me temper till it would be dethrimental to keep it. There's nothin' derogatory in th' use o' th' word " cuckoo," is there?

52

PETER (*tearfully*). It's not th' word; it's th' way he says it: he never says it straight out, but murmurs it with curious quiverin' ripples, like variations on a flute!

FLUTHER. Ah, what odds if he gave it with variations on a thrombone! (*To* MRS. GOGAN) What's yours goin' to be, maam?

MRS. GOGAN. Ah, a half o' malt, Fluther.

FLUTHER (*to* BARMAN). Three halves, Tommy.

(*The* BARMAN *brings the drinks.*)

MRS. GOGAN (*drinking*). The Foresthers' is a gorgeous dhress! I don't think I've seen nicer, mind you, in a pantomime. . . . Th' loveliest part of th' dhress, I think, is th' osthrichess plume. . . . When yous are goin' along, an' I see them wavin' an' noddin' an' waggin', I seem to be lookin' at each of yous hangin' at th' end of a rope, your eyes bulgin' an' your legs twistin' an' jerkin', gaspin' an' gaspin' for breath while yous are thryin' to die for Ireland!

FLUTHER. If any o' them is hangin' at the end of a rope, it won't be for Ireland!

PETER. Are you goin' to start th' young Covey's game o' proddin' an' twartin' a man? There's not many that's talkin' can say that for twenty-five years he never missed a pilgrimage to Bodenstown!

53

FLUTHER. You're always blowin' about goin' to Bodenstown. D'ye think no one but yourself ever went to Bodenstown?

PETER (*plaintively*). I'm not blowin' about it; but there's not a year that I go there but I pluck a leaf off Tone's grave, an' this very day me prayer-book is nearly full of them.

FLUTHER (*scornfully*). Then Fluther has a vice versa opinion of them that put ivy leaves into their prayer-books, scabbin' it on th' clergy, an' thryin' to out-do th' haloes o' th' saints be lookin' as if he was wearin' around his head a glittherin' aroree boree allis! (*Fiercely*) Sure, I don't care a damn if you slep' in Bodenstown! You can take your breakfast, dinner an' tea on th' grave, if you like, for Fluther!

MRS. GOGAN. Oh, don't start a fight, boys, for God's sake; I was only sayin' what a nice costume it is—nicer than th' kilts, for, God forgive me, I always think th' kilts is hardly decent.

FLUTHER. Ah, sure, when you'd look at him, you'd wondher whether th' man was makin' fun o' th' costume, or th' costume was makin' fun o' th' man!

BARMAN. Now, then, thry to speak asy, will yous? We don't want no shoutin' here.

(*The* COVEY *followed by* BESSIE BURGESS

come in. They go over to the opposite end of the counter, and direct their gaze on the other group.)

THE COVEY (*to* BARMAN). Two glasses o' malt.

PETER. There he is, now; I knew he wouldn't be long till he folleyed me in.

BESSIE (*speaking to the* COVEY, *but really at the other party*). I can't for th' life o' me undherstand how they can call themselves Catholics, when they won't lift a finger to help poor little Catholic Belgium.

MRS. GOGAN (*raising her voice*). What about poor little Catholic Ireland?

BESSIE (*over to* MRS. GOGAN). You mind your own business, maam, an' stupify your foolishness be gettin' dhrunk.

PETER (*anxiously*). Take no notice of her; pay no attention to her. She's just tormentin' herself towards havin' a row with somebody.

BESSIE. There's a storm of anger tossin' in me heart, thinkin' of all th' poor Tommies, an' with them me own son, dhrenched in water an' soaked in blood, gropin' their way to a shatther-in' death, in a shower o' shells! Young men with th' sunny lust o' life beamin' in them, layin' down their white bodies, shredded into torn an' bloody pieces, on th' althar that

55

God Himself has built for th' sacrifice of heroes!

MRS. GOGAN.   Isn't it a nice thing to have to be listenin' to a lassie an' hangin' our heads in a dead silence, knowin' that some persons think more of a ball of malt than they do of th' blessed saints.

FLUTHER.   Whisht; she's always dangerous an' derogatory when she's well oiled.   Th' safest way to hindher her from havin' any enjoyment out of her spite, is to dip our thoughts into the fact of her bein' a female person that has moved out of th' sight of ordinary sensible people.

BESSIE.   To look at some o' th' women that's knockin' about, now, is a thing to make a body sigh. . . . A woman on her own, dhrinkin' with a bevy o' men is hardly an example to her sex. . . . A woman dhrinkin' with a woman is one thing, an' a woman dhrinkin' with herself is still a woman—flappers may be put in another category altogether—but a middle-aged married woman makin' herself th' centre of a circle of men is as a woman that is loud an' stubborn, whose feet abideth not in her own house.

THE COVEY (*to* BESSIE).   When I think of all th' problems in front o' th' workers, it makes me sick to be lookin' at oul' codgers goin' about dhressed up like green-accoutered figures gone asthray out of a toyshop!

PETER. Gracious God, give me patience to be listenin' to that blasted young Covey proddin' at me from over at th' other end of th' shop!

MRS. GOGAN (*dipping her finger in the whisky, and moistening with it the lips of her baby*). Cissie Gogan's a woman livin' for nigh on twenty-five years in her own room, an' beyond biddin' th' time o' day to her neighbours, never yet as much as nodded her head in th' direction of other people's business, while she knows some as are never content unless they're standin' senthry over other people's doin's!

  (BESSIE *is about to reply, when the tall, dark figure is again silhouetted against the window, and the voice of the speaker is heard speaking passionately.*)

VOICE OF SPEAKER. The last sixteen months have been the most glorious in the history of Europe. Heroism has come back to the earth. War is a terrible thing, but war is not an evil thing. People in Ireland dread war because they do not know it. Ireland has not known the exhilaration of war for over a hundred years. When war comes to Ireland

57

she must welcome it as she would welcome the Angel of God!

(*The figure passes out of sight and hearing.*)

THE COVEY (*towards all present*). Dope, dope. There's only one war worth havin': th' war for th' economic emancipation of th' proletariat.

BESSIE. They may crow away out o' them; but it ud be fitther for some o' them to mend their ways, an' cease from havin' scouts out watchin' for th' comin' of th' Saint Vincent de Paul man, for fear they'd be nailed lowerin' a pint of beer, mockin' th' man with an angel face, shinin' with th' glamour of deceit an' lies!

MRS. GOGAN. An' a certain lassie standin' stiff behind her own door with her ears cocked listenin' to what's being said, stuffed till she's sthrained with envy of a neighbour thryin' for a few little things that may be got be hard sthrivin' to keep up to th' letther an' th' law, an' th' practices of th' Church!

PETER (*to* MRS. GOGAN). If I was you, Mrs. Gogan, I'd parry her jabbin' remarks be a powerful silence that'll keep her tantalizin' words from penethratin' into your feelin's. It's always betther to leave these people to th' vengeance o' God!

58

BESSIE. Bessie Burgess doesn't put up to know much, never havin' a swaggerin' mind, thanks be to God, but goin' on packin' up knowledge accordin' to her conscience: precept upon precept, line upon line; here a little, an' there a little. But (*with a passionate swing of her shawl*), thanks be to Christ, she knows when she was got, where she was got, an' how she was got; while there's some she knows, decoratin' their finger with a well-polished weddin' ring, would be hard put to it if they were assed to show their weddin' lines!

MRS. GOGAN (*plunging out into the centre of the floor in a wild tempest of hysterical rage*). Y' oul' rip of a blasted liar, me weddin' ring's been well earned be twenty years be th' side o' me husband, now takin' his rest in heaven, married to me be Father Dempsey, in th' Chapel o' Saint Jude's, in th' Christmas Week of eighteen hundhred an' ninety-five; an' any kid, livin' or dead, that Jinnie Gogan's had since, was got between th' bordhers of th' Ten Commandments! . . . An' that's more than some o' you can say that are kep' from th' dhread o' desthruction be a few drowsy virtues, that th' first whisper of temptation lulls into a sleep that'll know one sin from another only on th' day of their last anointin', an' that use th'

59

innocent light o' th' shinin' stars to dip into th' sins of a night's diversion!

BESSIE (*jumping out to face* MRS. GOGAN, *and bringing the palms of her hands together in sharp claps to emphasize her remarks*). Liar to you, too, maam, y' oul' hardened thresspasser on other people's good nature, wizenin' up your soul in th' arts o' dodgeries, till every dhrop of respectability in a female is dhried up in her, lookin' at your ready-made manœuverin' with th' menkind!

BARMAN. Here, there; here, there; speak asy there. No rowin' here, no rowin' here, now.

FLUTHER (*trying to calm* MRS. GOGAN). Now, Jinnie, Jinnie, it's a derogatory thing to be smirchin' a night like this with a row; it's rompin' with th' feelin's of hope we ought to be, instead o' bein' vice versa!

PETER (*trying to quiet* BESSIE). I'm terrible dawny, Mrs. Burgess, an' a fight leaves me weak for a long time afterwards. . . . Please, Mrs. Burgess, before there's damage done, thry to have a little respect for yourself.

BESSIE (*with a push of her hand that sends* PETER *tottering to the end of the shop*). G'way, you little sermonizing, little yella-faced, little consequential, little pudgy, little bum, you!

MRS. GOGAN (*screaming*). Fluther, leggo! I'm not goin' to keep an unresistin' silence, an' her scattherin' her festherin' words in me face, stirrin' up every dhrop of decency in a respectable female, with her restless rally o' lies that would make a saint say his prayer backwards!

BESSIE (*shouting*). Ah, everybody knows well that th' best charity that can be shown to you is to hide th' thruth as much as our thrue worship of God Almighty will allow us!

MRS. GOGAN (*frantically*). Here, houl' th' kid, one o' yous; houl' th' kid for a minute! There's nothin' for it but to show this lassie a lesson or two. . . . (*To* PETER) Here, houl' th' kid, you.

> (*Before* PETER *is aware of it, she places the infant in his arms.*)

MRS. GOGAN (*to* BESSIE, *standing before her in a fighting attitude*). Come on, now, me loyal lassie, dyin' with grief for little Catholic Belgium! When Jinnie Gogan's done with you, you'll have a little leisure lyin' down to think an' pray for your king an' counthry!

BARMAN (*coming from behind the counter, getting between the women, and proceeding to push them towards the door*). Here, now, since yous can't have a little friendly argument quietly, yous'll get out o' this place in quick time.

Go on, an' settle your differences somewhere else—I don't want to have another endorsement on me licence.

PETER (*anxiously, over to* MRS. GOGAN). Here, take your kid back, ower this. How nicely I was picked, now, for it to be plumped into me arms!

THE COVEY. She knew who she was givin' it to, maybe.

PETER (*hotly to the* COVEY). Now, I'm givin' you fair warnin', me young Covey, to quit firin' your jibes an' jeers at me. . . . For one o' these days, I'll run out in front o' God Almighty an' take your sacred life!

BARMAN (*pushing* BESSIE *out after* MRS. GOGAN). Go on, now; out you go.

BESSIE (*as she goes out*). If you think, me lassie, that Bessie Burgess has an untidy conscience, she'll soon show you to th' differ!

PETER (*leaving the baby down on the floor*). Ay, be Jasus, wait there, till I give her back her youngster! (*He runs to the door.*) Ay, there, ay! (*He comes back.*) There, she's afther goin' without her kid. What are we goin' to do with it, now?

THE COVEY. What are we goin' to do with it? Bring it outside an' show everybody what you're afther findin'!

62

PETER (*in a panic to* FLUTHER). Pick it up, you, Fluther, an' run afther her with it, will you?

FLUTHER. What d'ye take Fluther for? You must think Fluther's a right gom.   D'ye think Fluther's like yourself, destitute of a titther of undherstandin'?

BARMAN (*imperatively to* PETER). Take it up, man, an' run out afther her with it, before she's gone too far.   You're not goin' to leave th' bloody thing here, are you?

PETER (*plaintively, as he lifts up the baby*). Well, God Almighty, give me patience with all th' scorners, tormenters, an' twarters that are always an' ever thryin' to goad me into prayin' for their blindin' an' blastin' an' burnin' in th' world to come!

(*He goes out.*)

FLUTHER. God, it's a relief to get rid o' that crowd.   Women is terrible when they start to fight.   There's no holdin' them back. (*To the* COVEY) Are you goin' to have anything?

THE COVEY. Ah, I don't mind if I have another half.

FLUTHER (*to* BARMAN). Two more, Tommy, me son.

(*The* BARMAN *gets the drinks.*)

63

FLUTHER. You know, there's no conthrollin' a woman when she loses her head.

(ROSIE *enters and goes over to the counter on the side nearest to* FLUTHER.)

ROSIE (*to* BARMAN). Divil a use o' havin' a thrim little leg on a night like this; things was never worse. . . . Give us a half till to-morrow, Tom, duckey.

BARMAN (*coldly*). No more to-night, Rosie; you owe me for three already.

ROSIE (*combatively*). You'll be paid, won't you?

BARMAN. I hope so.

ROSIE. You hope so! Is that th' way with you, now?

FLUTHER (*to* BARMAN). Give her one; it'll be alright.

ROSIE (*clapping* FLUTHER *on the back*). Oul' sport!

FLUTHER. Th' meetin' should be soon over, now.

THE COVEY. Th' sooner th' betther. It's all a lot o' blasted nonsense, comrade.

FLUTHER. Oh, I wouldn't say it was all nonsense. Afther all, Fluther can remember th' time, an' him only a dawny chiselur, bein' taught at his mother's knee to be faithful to th' Shan Vok Vok!

64

THE COVEY. That's all dope, comrade; th' sort o' thing that workers are fed on be th' Boorzwawzee.

FLUTHER (*a little sharply*). What's all dope? Though I'm sayin' it that shouldn't: (*catching his cheek with his hand, and pulling down the flesh from the eye*) d'ye see that mark there, undher me eye? . . . A sabre slice from a dragoon in O'Connell Street! (*Thrusting his head forward towards* ROSIE) Feel that dint in th' middle o' me nut!

ROSIE (*rubbing* FLUTHER'S *head, and winking at the* COVEY). My God, there's a holla!

FLUTHER (*putting on his hat with quiet pride*). A skelp from a bobby's baton at a Labour meetin' in th' Phœnix Park!

THE COVEY. He must ha' hitten you in mistake. I don't know what you ever done for th' Labour movement.

FLUTHER (*loudly*). D'ye not? Maybe, then, I done as much, an' know as much about th' Labour movement as th' chancers that are blowin' about it!

BARMAN. Speak easy, Fluther, thry to speak easy.

THE COVEY. There's no necessity to get excited about it, comrade.

FLUTHER (*more loudly*). Excited? Who's

65   F

gettin' excited? There's no one gettin' excited! It would take something more than a thing like you to flutther a feather o' Fluther. Blatherin', an', when all is said, you know as much as th' rest in th' wind up!

THE COVEY. Well, let us put it to th' test, then, an' see what you know about th' Labour movement: what's the mechanism of exchange?

FLUTHER (*roaring, because he feels he is beaten*). How th' hell do I know what it is? There's nothin' about that in th' rules of our Thrades Union!

BARMAN. For God's sake, thry to speak easy, Fluther.

THE COVEY. What does Karl Marx say about th' Relation of Value to th' Cost o' Production?

FLUTHER (*angrily*). What th' hell do I care what he says? I'm Irishman enough not to lose me head be follyin' foreigners!

BARMAN. Speak easy, Fluther.

THE COVEY. It's only waste o' time talkin' to you, comrade.

FLUTHER. Don't be comradin' me, mate. I'd be on me last legs if I wanted you for a comrade.

ROSIE (*to the* COVEY). It seems a highly rediculous thing to hear a thing that's only an inch or two away from a kid, swingin' heavy words about he doesn't know th' meanin' of, an' uppishly thryin' to down a man like Misther Fluther here, that's well flavoured in th' knowledge of th' world he's livin' in.

THE COVEY (*savagely to* ROSIE). Nobody's askin' you to be buttin' in with your prate. . . . I have you well taped, me lassie. . . . Just you keep your opinions for your own place. . . . It'll be a long time before th' Covey takes any insthructions or reprimandin' from a prostitute!

ROSIE (*wild with humiliation*). You louse, you louse, you! . . . You're no man. . . . You're no man . . . I'm a woman, anyhow, an' if I'm a prostitute aself, I have me feelin's. . . . Thryin' to put his arm around me a minute ago, an' givin' me th' glad eye, th' little wrigglin' lump o' desolation turns on me now, because he saw there was nothin' doin'. . . . You louse, you! If I was a man, or you were a woman, I'd bate th' puss o' you!

BARMAN. Ay, Rosie, ay! You'll have to shut your mouth altogether, if you can't learn to speak easy!

FLUTHER (*to* ROSIE). Houl' on there, Rosie; houl' on there. There's no necessity to flutther yourself when you're with Fluther.

67

. . . Any lady that's in th' company of Fluther is goin' to get a fair hunt. . . . This is outside your province. . . . I'm not goin' to let you demean yourself be talkin' to a tittherin' chancer. . . . Leave this to Fluther—this is a man's job. (*To the* COVEY) Now, if you've anything to say, say it to Fluther, an', let me tell you, you're not goin' to be pass-remarkable to any lady in my company.

THE COVEY. Sure I don't care if you were runnin' all night afther your Mary o' th' Curlin' Hair, but, when you start tellin' luscious lies about what you done for th' Labour movement, it's nearly time to show y'up!

FLUTHER (*fiercely*). Is it you show Fluther up? G'way, man, I'd beat two o' you before me breakfast!

THE COVEY (*contemptuously*). Tell us where you bury your dead, will you?

FLUTHER (*with his face stuck into the face of the* COVEY). Sing a little less on th' high note, or, when I'm done with you, you'll put a Christianable consthruction on things, I'm tellin' you!

THE COVEY. You're a big fella, you are.

FLUTHER (*tapping the* COVEY *threateningly on the shoulder*). Now, you're temptin' Providence when you're temptin' Fluther!

THE COVEY (*losing his temper, and bawling*). Easy with them hands, there, easy with them hands! You're startin' to take a little risk when you commence to paw the Covey!

(FLUTHER *suddenly springs into the middle of the shop, flings his hat into the corner, whips off his coat, and begins to paw the air.*)

FLUTHER (*roaring at the top of his voice*). Come on, come on, you lowser; put your mits up now, if there's a man's blood in you! Be God, in a few minutes you'll see some snots flyin' around, I'm tellin' you. . . . When Fluther's done with you, you'll have a vice versa opinion of him! Come on, now, come on!

BARMAN (*running from behind the counter and catching hold of the* COVEY). Here, out you go, me little bowsey. Because you got a couple o' halves you think you can act as you like. (*He pushes the* COVEY *to the door*) Fluther's a friend o' mine, an' I'll not have him insulted.

THE COVEY (*struggling with the* BARMAN). Ay, leggo, leggo there; fair hunt, give a man a fair hunt! One minute with him is all I ask; one minute alone with him, while your runnin' for th' priest an' th' doctor!

FLUTHER (*to the* BARMAN). Let him go, let

69

him go, Tom: let him open th' door to sudden death if he wants to!

BARMAN (*to the* COVEY). Go on, out you go an' do th' bowsey somewhere else.

(*He pushes the* COVEY *out and comes back.*)

ROSIE (*getting* FLUTHER'S *hat as he is putting on his coat*). Be God, you put th' fear o' God in his heart that time! I thought you'd have to be dug out of him. . . . Th' way you lepped out without any of your fancy side-steppin'! " Men like Fluther," say I to meself, " is gettin' scarce nowadays."

FLUTHER (*with proud complacency*). I wasn't goin' to let meself be malignified by a chancer. . . . He got a little bit too derogatory for Fluther. . . . Be God, to think of a cur like that comin' to talk to a man like me!

ROSIE (*fixing on his hat*). Did j'ever!

FLUTHER. He's lucky he got off safe. I hit a man last week, Rosie, an' he's fallin' yet!

ROSIE. Sure, you'd ha' broken him in two if you'd ha' hitten him one clatther!

FLUTHER (*amorously, putting his arm around* ROSIE). Come on into th' snug, me little darlin', an' we'll have a few dhrinks before I see you home.

ROSIE. Oh, Fluther, I'm afraid you're a terrible man for th' women.

70

(They go into the snug as CLITHEROE, CAPTAIN BRENNAN *and* LIEUT. LANGON *of the Irish Volunteers enter hurriedly.* CAPTAIN BRENNAN *carries the banner of The Plough and the Stars, and* LIEUT. LANGON *a green, white and orange Tri-colour. They are in a state of emotional excitement. Their faces are flushed and their eyes sparkle; they speak rapidly, as if unaware of the meaning of what they said. They have been mesmerized by the fervency of the speeches.)*

CLITHEROE *(almost pantingly).* Three glasses o' port!

(The BARMAN *brings the drinks.)*

CAPT. BRENNAN. We won't have long to wait now.

LIEUT. LANGON. Th' time is rotten ripe for revolution.

CLITHEROE. You have a mother, Langon.

LIEUT. LANGON. Ireland is greater than a mother.

CAPT. BRENNAN. You have a wife, Clitheroe.

CLITHEROE. Ireland is greater than a wife.

LIEUT. LANGON. Th' time for Ireland's battle is now — th' place for Ireland's battle is here.

71

(*The tall, dark figure again is silhouetted against the window. The three men pause and listen.*)

VOICE OF THE MAN. Our foes are strong, but strong as they are, they cannot undo the miracles of God, who ripens in the heart of young men the seeds sown by the young men of a former generation. They think they have pacified Ireland; think they have foreseen everything; think they have provided against everything; but the fools, the fools, the fools! —they have left us our Fenian dead, and, while Ireland holds these graves, Ireland, unfree, shall never be at peace!

CAPT. BRENNAN (*catching up The Plough and the Stars*). Imprisonment for th' Independence of Ireland!

LIEUT. LANGON (*catching up the Tri-colour*). Wounds for th' Independence of Ireland!

CLITHEROE. Death for th' Independence of Ireland!

THE THREE (*together*). So help us God!

(*They drink. A bugle blows the Assembly. They hurry out. A pause.* FLUTHER *and* ROSIE *come out of the snug;* ROSIE *is linking* FLUTHER, *who is a little drunk. Both are in a merry mood.*)

ROSIE. Come on home, ower o' that, man.

72

Are you afraid or what? Are you goin' to come home, or are you not?

FLUTHER. Of course I'm goin' home. What ud ail me that I wouldn't go?

ROSIE (*lovingly*). Come on, then, oul' sport.

OFFICER'S VOICE (*giving command outside*). Irish Volunteers, by th' right, quick march!

ROSIE (*putting her arm round* FLUTHER *and singing*):

I once had a lover, a tailor, but he could do nothin'
    for me,
An' then I fell in with a sailor as strong an' as wild
    as th' sea.
We cuddled an' kissed with devotion, till th' night
    from th' mornin' had fled;
An' there, to our joy, a bright bouncin' boy
Was dancin' a jig in th' bed!

Dancin' a jig in th' bed, an' bawlin' for butther an'
    bread.
An' there, to our joy, a bright bouncin' boy
Was dancin' a jig in th' bed!

> (*They go out with their arms round each
>   other.*)

CLITHEROE'S VOICE (*in command outside*). Dublin Battalion of the Irish Citizen Army, by th' right, quick march!

CURTAIN

73

ACT III

(The corner house in a street of tenements: it is the home of the CLITHEROES. *The house is a long, gaunt, five-story tenement; its brick front is chipped and scarred with age and neglect. The wide and heavy hall door, flanked by two pillars, has a look of having been charred by a fire in the distant past. The door lurches a little to one side, disjointed by the continual and reckless banging when it is being closed by most of the residents. The diamond-paned fan-light is destitute of a single pane, the frame-work alone remaining. The windows, except the two looking into the front parlour (*CLITHEROE'S *room), are grimy, and are draped with fluttering and soiled fragments of lace curtains. The front parlour windows are hung with rich, comparatively, casement cloth. Five stone steps lead from the door to the path on the street. Branching on each side are railings to prevent*

74

*people from falling into the area. At the
left corner of the house runs a narrow lane,
bisecting the street, and connecting it with
another of the same kind. At the corner of
the lane is a street lamp.*

As the house is revealed, MRS. GOGAN *is seen
helping* MOLLSER *to a chair, which stands on
the path beside the railings, at the left side of
the steps. She then wraps a shawl around*
MOLLSER'S *shoulders. It is some months
later.)*

MRS. GOGAN (*arranging shawl around* MOLLSER).
Th' sun'll do you all th' good in th' world. A
few more weeks o' this weather, an' there's no
knowin' how well you'll be. . . . Are you
comfy, now?

MOLLSER (*weakly and wearily*). Yis, ma;
I'm alright.

MRS. GOGAN. How are you feelin'?

MOLLSER. Betther, ma, betther. If th'
horrible sinkin' feelin' ud go, I'd be alright.

MRS. GOGAN. Ah, I wouldn't put much
pass on that. Your stomach, maybe's out of
ordher. . . . Is th' poor breathin' any betther,
d'ye think?

MOLLSER. Yis, yis, ma; a lot betther.

MRS. GOGAN. Well, that's somethin' anyhow. . . . With th' help o' God, you'll be on th' mend from this out. . . . D'your legs feel any sthronger undher you, d'ye think?

MOLLSER (*irritably*). I can't tell, ma. I think so. . . . A little.

MRS. GOGAN. Well, a little aself is somethin'. . . . I thought I heard you coughin' a little more than usual last night. . . . D'ye think you were?

MOLLSER. I wasn't, ma, I wasn't.

MRS. GOGAN. I thought I heard you, for I was kep' awake all night with th' shootin'. An' thinkin' o' that madman, Fluther, runnin' about through th' night lookin' for Nora Clitheroe to bring her back when he heard she'd gone to folly her husband, an' in dhread any minute he might come staggerin' in covered with bandages, splashed all over with th' red of his own blood, an' givin' us barely time to bring th' priest to hear th' last whisper of his final confession, as his soul was passin' through th' dark doorway o' death into th' way o' th' wondherin' dead. . . . You don't feel cold, do you?

MOLLSER. No, ma; I'm alright.

MRS. GOGAN. Keep your chest well covered, for that's th' delicate spot in you . . . if there's any danger, I'll whip you in again. . . .

(*Looking up the street*) Oh, here's th' Covey an' oul' Pether hurryin' along. God Almighty, sthrange things is happenin' when them two is pullin' together.

(*The* COVEY *and* PETER *come in, breathless and excited.*)

MRS. GOGAN (*to the two men*). Were yous far up th' town? Did yous see any sign o' Fluther or Nora? How is things lookin'? I hear they're blazin' away out o' th' G.P.O. That th' Tommies is sthretched in heaps around Nelson's Pillar an' th' Parnell Statue, an' that th' pavin' sets in O'Connell Street is nearly covered be pools o' blood.

PETER. We seen no sign o' Nora or Fluther anywhere.

MRS. GOGAN. We should ha' held her back be main force from goin' to look for her husband. . . . God knows what's happened to her—I'm always seein' her sthretched on her back in some hospital, moanin' with th' pain of a bullet in her vitals, an' nuns thryin' to get her to take a last look at th' crucifix!

THE COVEY. We can do nothin'. You can't stick your nose into O'Connell Street, an' Tyler's is on fire.

PETER. An' we seen th' Lancers——

THE COVEY (*interrupting*). Throttin' along,

77

heads in th' air; spurs an' sabres jinglin', an' lances quiverin', an' lookin' as if they were assin' themselves, " Where's these blighters, till we get a prod at them," when there was a volley from th' Post Office that stretched half o' them, an' sent th' rest gallopin' away wondherin' how far they'd have to go before they'd feel safe.

PETER (*rubbing his hands*). " Damn it," says I to meself, " this looks like business! "

THE COVEY. An' then out comes General Pearse an' his staff, an', standin' in th' middle o' th' street, he reads th' Proclamation.

MRS. GOGAN. What proclamation?

PETER. Declarin' an Irish Republic.

MRS. GOGAN. Go to God!

PETER. The gunboat *Helga's* shellin' Liberty Hall, an' I hear that people livin' on th' quays had to crawl on their bellies to Mass with th' bullets that were flyin' around from Boland's Mills.

MRS. GOGAN. God bless us, what's goin' to be th' end of it all!

BESSIE (*looking out of the top window*). Maybe yous are satisfied now; maybe yous are satisfied now! Go on an' get guns if yous are men— Johnny get your gun, get your gun, get your gun! Yous are all nicely shanghaied now;

th' boyo hasn't a sword on his thigh, now!   Oh, yous are all nicely shanghaied now!

MRS. GOGAN (*warningly to* PETER *and the* COVEY). S-s-sh, don't answer her.   She's th' right oul' Orange bitch!   She's been chantin' " Rule, Britannia " all th' mornin'.

PETER. I hope Fluther hasn't met with any accident, he's such a wild card.

THE COVEY. Fluther's well able to take care of himself.

MRS. GOGAN. God grant it; but last night I dreamt I seen gettin' carried into th' house a sthretcher with a figure lyin' on it, stiff an' still, dhressed in th' habit of Saint Francis. An' then, I heard th' murmurs of a crowd no one could see sayin' th' litany for th' dead; an' then it got so dark that nothin' was seen but th' white face of th' corpse, gleamin' like a white wather lily floatin' on th' top of a dark lake.   Then a tiny whisper thrickled into me ear, sayin', " Isn't the face very like th' face o' Fluther," an' then, with a thremblin' flutther, th' dead lips opened, an', although I couldn't hear, I knew they were sayin', " Poor oul' Fluther, afther havin' handin' in his gun at last, his shakin' soul moored in th' place where th' wicked are at rest an' th' weary cease from throublin'."

79

PETER (*who has put on a pair of spectacles, and has been looking down the street*). Here they are, be God, here they are; just afther turnin' th' corner—Nora an' Fluther!

THE COVEY. She must be wounded or something—he seems to be carryin' her.

> (FLUTHER *and* NORA *enter.* FLUTHER *has his arm around her and is half leading, half carrying her in. Her eyes are dim and hollow, her face pale and strained looking; her hair is tossed, and her clothes are dusty.*)

MRS. GOGAN (*running over to them*). God bless us, is it wounded y'are Mrs. Clitheroe, or what?

FLUTHER. Ah, she's all right, Mrs. Gogan; only worn out from thravellin' an' want o' sleep. A night's rest, now, an' she'll be as fit as a fiddle. Bring her in, an' make her lie down.

MRS. GOGAN (*to* NORA). Did you hear e'er a whisper o' Mr. Clitheroe?

NORA (*wearily*). I could find him nowhere, Mrs. Gogan. None o' them would tell me where he was. They told me I shamed my husband an' th' women of Ireland be carryin' on as I was. . . . They said th' women must learn to be brave an' cease to be cowardly. . . .

Me who risked more for love than they would risk for hate. . . . (*Raising her voice in hysterical protest*) My Jack will be killed, my Jack will be killed! . . . He is to be butchered as a sacrifice to th' dead!

BESSIE (*from upper window*). Yous are all nicely shanghaied now! Sorra mend th' lasses that have been kissin' an' cuddlin' their boys into th' sheddin' of blood! . . . Fillin' their minds with fairy tales that had no beginnin', but, please God, 'll have a bloody quick endin'! . . . Turnin' bitther into sweet, an' sweet into bitther. . . . Stabbin' in th' back th' men that are dyin' in th' threnches for them! It's a bad thing for any one that thrys to jilt th' Ten Commandments, for judgements are prepared for scorners an' sthripes for th' back o' fools! (*Going away from window as she sings*):

Rule, Britannia, Britannia rules th' waves,
Britons never, never, never shall be slaves!

FLUTHER (*with a roar up at the window*). Y'ignorant oul' throllope, you!

MRS. GOGAN (*to* NORA). He'll come home safe enough to you, you'll find, Mrs. Clitheroe; afther all, there's a power o' women that's handed over sons an' husbands to take a runnin'-risk in th' fight they're wagin'.

81   G

NORA. I can't help thinkin' every shot fired 'll be fired at Jack, an' every shot fired at Jack 'll be fired at me. What do I care for th' others? I can think only of me own self. . . . An' there's no woman gives a son or a husband to be killed—if they say it, they're lyin', lyin', against God, Nature, an' against themselves! . . . One blasted hussy at a barricade told me to go home an' not be thryin' to dishearten th' men. . . . That I wasn't worthy to bear a son to a man that was out fightin' for freedom. . . . I clawed at her, an' smashed her in th' face till we were separated. . . . I was pushed down th' street, an' I cursed them—cursed the rebel ruffians an' Volunteers that had dhragged me ravin' mad into th' sthreets to seek me husband!

PETER. You'll have to have patience, Nora. We all have to put up with twarthers an' tormentors in this world.

THE COVEY. If they were fightin' for anything worth while, I wouldn't mind.

FLUTHER (to NORA). Nothin' derogatory 'll happen to Mr. Clitheroe. You'll find, now, in th' finish up, it'll be vice versa.

NORA. Oh, I know that wherever he is, he's thinkin' of wantin' to be with me. I know he's longin' to be passin' his hand through me hair, to be caressin' me neck, to fondle me hand an' to feel me kisses clingin' to his mouth. . . . An' he stands wherever he is because he's brave? (*Vehemently*) No, but because he's a coward, a coward, a coward!

MRS. GOGAN. Oh, they're not cowards anyway.

NORA (*with denunciatory anger*). I tell you they're afraid to say they're afraid! . . . Oh, I saw it, I saw it, Mrs. Gogan. . . . At th' barricade in North King Street I saw fear glowin' in all their eyes. . . . An' in th' middle o' th' sthreet was somethin' huddled up in a horrible tangled heap. . . . His face was jammed again th' stones, an' his arm was twisted round his back. . . . An' every twist of his body was a cry against th' terrible thing that had happened to him. . . . An' I saw they were afraid to look at it. . . . An' some o' them laughed at me, but th' laugh was a frightened one. . . . An' some o' them shouted at me, but th' shout had in it th' shiver o' fear. . . . I tell you they were afraid, afraid, afraid!

MRS. GOGAN (*leading her towards the house*). Come on in, dear. If you'd been a little longer together, th' wrench asundher wouldn't have been so sharp.

83

NORA. Th' agony I'm in since he left me has thrust away every rough thing he done, an' every unkind word he spoke; only th' blossoms that grew out of our lives are before me now; shakin' their colours before me face, an' breathin' their sweet scent on every thought springin' up in me mind, till, sometimes, Mrs. Gogan, sometimes I think I'm goin' mad!

MRS. GOGAN. You'll be a lot betther when you have a little lie down.

NORA (*turning towards* FLUTHER *as she is going in*). I don't know what I'd have done, only for Fluther. I'd have been lyin' in th' streets, only for him. . . . (*As she goes in*) They have dhriven away th' little happiness life had to spare for me. He has gone from me for ever, for ever. . . . Oh, Jack, Jack, Jack!

> (*She is led in by* MRS. GOGAN *as* BESSIE
> *comes out with a shawl around her*
> *shoulders. She passes by them with*
> *her head in the air. When they have*
> *gone in, she gives a mug of milk to*
> MOLLSER *silently*.)

FLUTHER. Which of yous has th' tossers?

THE COVEY. I have.

BESSIE (*as she is passing them to go down the street*). You an' your Leadhers an' their sham-battle soldiers has landed a body in a nice way, havin' to go an' ferret out a bit o' bread God knows where. . . . Why aren't yous in th' G.P.O. if yous are men? It's paler an' paler yous are gettin'. . . . A lot o' vipers, that's what th' Irish people is!

(*She goes out.*)

FLUTHER. Never mind her. . . . (*To the* COVEY) Make a start an' keep us from th' sin o' idleness. (*To* MOLLSER.) Well, how are you to-day, Mollser, oul' son? What are you dhrinkin', milk?

MOLLSER. Grand, Fluther, grand, thanks. Yis, milk.

FLUTHER. You couldn't get a betther thing down you. . . . This turn-up has done one good thing, anyhow; you can't get dhrink anywhere, an' if it lasts a week, I'll be so used to it that I won't think of a pint.

THE COVEY (*who has taken from his pocket two worn coins and a thin strip of wood about four inches long*). What's th' bettin'?

PETER. Heads, a juice.

FLUTHER. Harps, a tanner.

(*The* COVEY *places the coins on the strip of wood, and flips them up into the air. As they jingle on the ground the distant boom of a big gun is heard. They stand for a moment listening.*)

85

FLUTHER. What th' hell's that?

THE COVEY. It's like th' boom of a big gun!

FLUTHER. Surely to God they're not goin' to use artillery on us?

THE COVEY (*scornfully*). Not goin'! (*Vehemently*) Wouldn't they use anything on us, man?

FLUTHER. Aw, holy Christ, that's not playin' th' game!

PETER (*plaintively*). What would happen if a shell landed here now?

THE COVEY (*ironically*). You'd be off to heaven in a fiery chariot.

PETER. In spite of all th' warnin's that's ringin' around us, are you goin' to start your pickin' at me again?

FLUTHER. Go on, toss them again, toss them again. . . . Harps, a tanner.

PETER. Heads, a juice.

(*The* COVEY *tosses the coins.*)

FLUTHER (*as the coins fall*). Let them roll, let them roll.   Heads, be God!

(BESSIE *runs in excitedly.   She has a new hat on her head, a fox fur round her neck, over her shawl, three umbrellas under her right arm, and a box of biscuits under her left.   She speaks rapidly and breathlessly.*)

86

BESSIE. They're breakin' into th' shops, they're breakin' into th' shops! Smashin' th' windows, battherin' in th' doors an' whippin' away everything! An' th' Volunteers is firin' on them. I seen two men an' a lassie pushin' a piano down th' sthreet, an' th' sweat rollin' off them thryin' to get it up on th' pavement; an' an oul' wan that must ha' been seventy lookin' as if she'd dhrop every minute with th' dint o' heart beatin', thryin' to pull a big double bed out of a broken shop window! I was goin' to wait till I dhressed meself from th' skin out.

MOLLSER (*to* BESSIE, *as she is going in*). Help me in, Bessie; I'm feelin' curious.

(BESSIE *leaves the looted things in the house, and, rapidly returning, helps* MOLLSER *in.*)

THE COVEY. Th' selfishness of that one—she waited till she got all she could carry before she'd come to tell any one!

FLUTHER (*running over to the door of the house and shouting in to* BESSIE). Ay, Bessie, did you hear of e'er a pub gettin' a shake up?

BESSIE (*inside*). I didn't hear o' none.

FLUTHER (*in a burst of enthusiasm*). Well, you're goin' to hear of one soon!

THE COVEY. Come on, man, an' don't be wastin' time.

87

PETER (*to them as they are about to run off*). Ay, ay, are yous goin' to leave me here?

FLUTHER. Are you goin' to leave yourself here?

PETER (*anxiously*). Didn't yous hear her sayin' they were firin' on them?

THE COVEY *and* FLUTHER (*together*). Well?

PETER. Supposin' I happened to be potted?

FLUTHER. We'd give you a Christian burial, anyhow.

THE COVEY (*ironically*). Dhressed up in your regimentals.

PETER (*to the* COVEY, *passionately*). May th' all-lovin' God give you a hot knock one o' these days, me young Covey, tuthorin' Fluther up now to be tiltin' at me, an' crossin' me with his mockeries an' jibin'!

> (*A fashionably dressed, middle-aged, stout woman comes hurriedly in, and makes for the group. She is almost fainting with fear.*)

THE WOMAN. For Gawd's sake, will one of you kind men show any safe way for me to get to Wrathmines? . . . I was foolish enough to visit a friend, thinking the howl thing was a joke, and now I cawn't get a car or a tram to take me home—isn't it awful?

FLUTHER. I'm afraid, ma'am, one way is as safe as another.

WOMAN. And what am I gowing to do? Oh, isn't this awful? . . . I'm so different from others. . . . The mowment I hear a shot, my legs give way under me—I cawn't stir, I'm paralysed—isn't it awful?

FLUTHER (*moving away*). It's a derogatory way to be, right enough, ma'am.

WOMAN (*catching* FLUTHER's *coat*). Creeping along the street there, with my head down and my eyes half shut, a bullet whizzed past within an inch of my nowse. . . . I had to lean against the wall for a long time, gasping for breath— I nearly passed away—it was awful! . . . I wonder, would you kind men come some of the way and see me safe?

FLUTHER. I have to go away, ma'am, to thry an' save a few things from th' burnin' buildin's.

THE COVEY. Come on, then, or there won't be anything left to save.

(*The* COVEY *and* FLUTHER *hurry away*.)

WOMAN (*to* PETER). Wasn't it an awful thing for me to leave my friend's house? Wasn't it an idiotic thing to do? . . . I haven't the slightest idea where I am. . . . You have a kind face, sir. Could you possibly come and pilot me in the direction of Wrathmines?

PETER (*indignantly*). D'ye think I'm goin' to risk me life throttin' in front of you? An' maybe get a bullet that would gimme a game leg or something that would leave me a jibe an' a jeer to Fluther an' th' young Covey for th' rest o' me days!

(*With an indignant toss of his head he walks into the house.*)

THE WOMAN (*going out*). I know I'll fall down in a dead faint if I hear another shot go off anyway near me—isn't it awful?

(MRS. GOGAN *comes out of the house pushing a pram before her. As she enters the street,* BESSIE *rushes out, follows* MRS. GOGAN, *and catches hold of the pram, stopping* MRS. GOGAN'S *progress.*)

BESSIE. Here, where are you goin' with that? How quick you were, me lady, to clap your eyes on th' pram. . . . Maybe you don't know that Mrs. Sullivan, before she went to spend Easther with her people in Dunboyne, gave me sthrict injunctions to give an accasional look to see if it was still standin' where it was left in th' corner of th' lobby.

MRS. GOGAN. That remark of yours, Mrs. Bessie Burgess, requires a little considheration, seein' that th' pram was left on our lobby, an' not on yours; a foot or two a little to th' left of th' jamb of me own room door; nor is it needful to mention th' name of th' person that gave a squint to see if it was there th' first thing in th' mornin', an' th' last thing in th' stillness o' th' night; never failin' to realize that her eyes couldn't be goin' wrong, be sthretchin' out her arm an' runnin' her hand over th' pram, to make sure that th' sight was no deception! Moreover, somethin's tellin' me that th' runnin' hurry of an inthrest you're takin' in it now is a sudden ambition to use th' pram for a purpose, that a loyal woman of law an' ordher would stagger away from!

> (*She gives the pram a sudden push that pulls* BESSIE *forward.*)

BESSIE (*still holding the pram*). There's not as much as one body in th' house that doesn't know that it wasn't Bessie Burgess that was always shakin' her voice complainin' about people leavin' bassinettes in th' way of them that, week in an' week out, had to pay their rent, an' always had to find a regular accommodation for her own furniture in her own room. . . . An' as for law an' ordher, puttin' aside th' harp an' shamrock, Bessie Burgess 'll have as much respect as she wants for th' lion an' unicorn!

PETER (*appearing at the door*). I think I'll go

with th' pair of yous an' see th' fun. A fella
might as well chance it, anyhow.

MRS. GOGAN (*taking no notice of* PETER, *and
pushing the pram on another step*). Take your
rovin' lumps o' hands from pattin' th' bassinette,
if you please, ma'am; an', steppin' from th'
threshold of good manners, let me tell you, Mrs.
Burgess, that's it's a fat wondher to Jennie
Gogan that a lady-like singer o' hymns like
yourself would lower her thoughts from sky-
thinkin' to sthretch out her arm in a sly-seekin'
way to pinch anything dhriven asthray in th'
confusion of th' battle our boys is makin' for
th' freedom of their counthry!

PETER (*laughing and rubbing his hands together*).
Hee, hee, hee, hee, hee! I'll go with th' pair
o' yous an' give yous a hand.

MRS. GOGAN (*with a rapid turn of her head
as she shoves the pram forward*). Get up in th'
prambulator an' we'll wheel you down.

BESSIE (*to* MRS. GOGAN). Poverty an' hard-
ship has sent Bessie Burgess to abide with
sthrange company, but she always knew them
she had to live with from backside to breakfast
time; an' she can tell them, always havin' had
a Christian kinch on her conscience, that a
passion for thievin' an' pinchin' would find her
soul a foreign place to live in, an' that her

92

present intention is quite th' lofty-hearted one of pickin' up anything shaken up an' scatthered about in th' loose confusion of a general plundher!

> (*By this time they have disappeared from view.* PETER *is following when the boom of a big gun in the distance brings him to a quick halt.*)

PETER. God Almighty, that's th' big gun again! God forbid any harm would happen to them, but sorra mind I'd mind if they met with a dhrop in their mad endeyvours to plundher an' desthroy.

> (*He looks down the street for a moment, then runs to the hall door of the house, which is open, and shuts it with a vicious pull; he then goes to the chair in which* MOLLSER *had sat, sits down, takes out his pipe, lights it and begins to smoke with his head carried at a haughty angle. The* COVEY *comes staggering in with a ten-stone sack of flour on his back. On the top of the sack is a ham. He goes over to the door, pushes it with his head, and finds he can't open it; he turns slightly in the direction of* PETER.)

THE COVEY (*to* PETER). Who shut th' door?

. . . (*He kicks at it*) Here, come on an' open it, will you?   This isn't a mot's hand-bag I've got on me back.

PETER. Now, me young Covey, d'ye think I'm goin' to be your lackey?

THE COVEY (*angrily*). Will you open th' door, y'oul——

PETER (*shouting*). Don't be assin' me to open any door, don't be assin' me to open any door for you. . . . Makin' a shame an' a sin o' th' cause that good men are fightin' for. . . . Oh, God forgive th' people that, instead o' burnishin' th' work th' boys is doin' to-day, with quiet honesty an' patience, is revilin' their sacrifices with a riot of lootin' an' roguery!

THE COVEY. Isn't your own eyes leppin' out o' your head with envy that you haven't th' guts to ketch a few o' th' things that God is givin' to His chosen people? . . . Y'oul hypocrite, if every one was blind you'd steal a cross off an ass's back!

PETER (*very calmly*). You're not goin' to make me lose me temper; you can go on with your proddin' as long as you like; goad an' goad an' goad away; hee hee, heee! I'll not lose me temper.

(*Somebody opens door and the* COVEY *goes in.*)

94

THE COVEY (*inside, mockingly*). Cuckoo-oo!

PETER (*running to the door and shouting in a blaze of passion as he follows the* COVEY *in*). You lean, long, lanky, lath of a lowsey bastard. . . . (*Following him in*) Lowsey bastard, lowsey bastard!

> (BESSIE *and* MRS. GOGAN *enter, the pride of a great joy illuminating their faces.* BESSIE *is pushing the pram, which is filled with clothes and boots; on the top of the boots and clothes is a fancy table, which* MRS. GOGAN *is holding on with her left hand, while with her right hand she holds a chair on the top of her head. They are heard talking to each other before they enter.*)

MRS. GOGAN (*outside*). I don't remember ever havin' seen such lovely pairs as them, (*they appear*) with th' pointed toes an' th' cuban heels.

BESSIE. They'll go grand with th' dhresses we're afther liftin', when we've stitched a sthray bit o' silk to lift th' bodices up a little bit higher, so as to shake th' shame out o' them, an' make them fit for women that hasn't lost themselves in th' nakedness o' th' times.

> (*They fussily carry in the chair, the table and some of the other goods. They return to bring in the rest.*)

95

PETER (*at door, sourly to* MRS. GOGAN). Ay, you. Mollser looks as if she was goin' to faint, an' your youngster is roarin' in convulsions in her lap.

MRS. GOGAN (*snappily*). She's never any other way but faintin'!

(*She goes to go in with some things in her arms, when a shot from a rifle rings out. She and* BESSIE *make a bolt for the door, which* PETER, *in a panic, tries to shut before they have got inside.*)

MRS. GOGAN. Ay, ay, ay, you cowardly oul' fool, what are you thryin' to shut th' door on us for?

(*They retreat tumultuously inside. A pause; then* CAPTAIN BRENNAN *comes in supporting* LIEUTENANT LANGON, *whose arm is around* BRENNAN'S *neck.* LANGON'S *face, which is ghastly white, is momentarily convulsed with spasms of agony. He is in a state of collapse, and* BRENNAN *is almost carrying him. After a few moments* CLITHEROE, *pale, and in a state of calm nervousness, follows, looking back in the direction from which he came, a rifle, held at the ready, in his hands.*)

96

CAPT. BRENNAN (*savagely to* CLITHEROE). Why did you fire over their heads? Why didn't you fire to kill?

CLITHEROE. No, no, Bill; bad as they are they're Irishmen an' women.

CAPT. BRENNAN (*savagely*). Irish be damned! Attackin' an' mobbin' th' men that are riskin' their lives for them. If these slum lice gather at our heels again, plug one o' them, or I'll soon shock them with a shot or two meself!

LIEUT. LANGON (*moaningly*). My God, is there ne'er an ambulance knockin' around anywhere? . . . Th' stomach is ripped out o' me; I feel it—o-o-oh, Christ!

CAPT. BRENNAN. Keep th' heart up, Jim; we'll soon get help, now.

> (NORA *rushes wildly out of the house and flings her arms round the neck of* CLITHEROE *with a fierce and joyous insistence. Her hair is down, her face is haggard, but her eyes are agleam with the light of happy relief.*)

NORA. Jack, Jack, Jack; oh, God be thanked . . . be thanked. . . . He has been kind and merciful to His poor handmaiden. . . . My Jack, my own Jack, that I thought was lost is found, that I thought was dead is alive again! . . . Oh, God be praised for ever,

evermore! . . . My poor Jack. . . . Kiss me,
kiss me, Jack, kiss your own Nora!

CLITHEROE (*kissing her, and speaking brokenly*).
My Nora; my little, beautiful Nora, I wish to
God, I'd never left you.

NORA. It doesn't matter—not now, not
now, Jack. It will make us dearer than
ever to each other. . . . Kiss me, kiss me
again.

CLITHEROE. Now, for God's sake, Nora,
don't make a scene.

NORA. I won't, I won't; I promise, I
promise, Jack; honest to God. I'll be silent
an' brave to bear th' joy of feelin' you safe in
my arms again. . . . It's hard to force away
th' tears of happiness at th' end of an awful
agony.

BESSIE (*from the upper window*). Th' Mins-
threl Boys aren't feelin' very comfortable now.
Th' big guns has knocked all th' harps out of
their hands. General Clitheroe 'd rather be
unlacin' his wife's bodice than standin' at a
barricade. . . . An' th' professor of chicken-
butcherin' there, finds he's up against somethin'
a little tougher even than his own chickens, an'
that's sayin' a lot!

CAPT. BRENNAN (*up to* BESSIE). Shut up,
y'oul hag!

BESSIE (*down to* BRENNAN). Choke th' chicken, choke th' chicken, choke th' chicken!

LIEUT. LANGON. For God's sake, Bill, bring me some place where me wound 'll be looked afther. . . . Am I to die before anything is done to save me?

CAPT. BRENNAN (*to* CLITHEROE). Come on, Jack. We've got to get help for Jim, here —have you no thought for his pain an' danger?

BESSIE. Choke th' chicken, choke th' chicken, choke th' chicken!

CLITHEROE (*to* NORA). Loosen me, darling, let me go.

NORA. (*clinging to him*). No, no, no, I'll not let you go! Come on, come up to our home, Jack, my sweetheart, my lover, my husband, an' we'll forget th' last few terrible days! . . . I look tired now, but a few hours of happy rest in your arms will bring back th' bloom of freshness again, an' you will be glad, you will be glad, glad . . . glad!

LIEUT. LANGON. Oh, if I'd kep' down only a little longer, I mightn't ha' been hit! Every one else escapin', an' me gettin' me belly ripped asundher! . . . I couldn't scream, couldn't even scream. . . . D'ye think I'm really badly wounded, Bill? Me clothes seem to be all soakin' wet. . . . It's blood . . . My God, it must be me own blood!

CAPT. BRENNAN (*to* CLITHEROE). Go on, Jack, bid her good-bye with another kiss, an' be done with it! D'ye want Langon to die in me arms while you're dallyin' with your Nora?

CLITHEROE (*to* NORA). I must go, I must go, Nora. I'm sorry we met at all. . . . It couldn't be helped—all other ways were blocked be th' British. . . . Let me go, can't you, Nora? D'ye want me to be unthrue to me comrades?

NORA. No, I won't let you go. . . . I want you to be thrue to me, Jack. . . . I'm your dearest comrade; I'm your thruest comrade. . . . They only want th' comfort of havin' you in th' same danger as themselves. . . . Oh, Jack, I can't let you go!

CLITHEROE. You must, Nora, you must.

NORA. All last night at th' barricades I sought you, Jack. . . . I didn't think of th' danger—I could only think of you. . . . I asked for you everywhere. . . . Some o' them laughed. . . . I was pushed away, but I shoved back. . . . Some o' them even sthruck me. . . . an' I screamed an' screamed your name!

CLITHEROE (*in fear her action would give him*

future shame). What possessed you to make a show of yourself, like that? . . . What way d'ye think I'll feel when I'm told my wife was bawlin' for me at th' barricades? What are you more than any other woman?

NORA. No more, maybe; but you are more to me than any other man, Jack. . . . I didn't mean any harm, honestly, Jack. . . . I couldn't help it. . . . I shouldn't have told you. . . . My love for you made me mad with terror.

CLITHEROE (*angrily*). They'll say now that I sent you out th' way I'd have an excuse to bring you home. . . . Are you goin' to turn all th' risks I'm takin' into a laugh?

LIEUT. LANGON. Let me lie down, let me lie down, Bill; th' pain would be easier, maybe, lyin' down. . . . Oh, God, have mercy on me!

CAPT. BRENNAN (*to* LANGON). A few steps more, Jim, a few steps more; thry to stick it for a few steps more.

LIEUT. LANGON. Oh, I can't, I can't, I can't!

CAPT. BRENNAN (*to* CLITHEROE). Are you comin', man, or are you goin' to make an arrangement for another honeymoon. . . . If you want to act th' renegade, say so, an' we'll be off!

BESSIE (*from above*). Runnin' from th'

Tommies—choke th' chicken. Runnin' from th' Tommies—choke th' chicken!

CLITHEROE (*savagely to* BRENNAN). Damn you, man, who wants to act th' renegade? (*To* NORA) Here, let go your hold; let go, I say!

NORA (*clinging to* CLITHEROE, *and indicating* BRENNAN). Look, Jack, look at th' anger in his face; look at th' fear glintin' in his eyes. . . . He, himself's afraid, afraid, afraid! . . . He wants you to go th' way he'll have th' chance of death sthrikin' you an' missin' him! . . . Turn round an' look at him, Jack, look at him, look at him! . . . His very soul is cold . . . shiverin' with th' thought of what may happen to him. . . . It is his fear that is thryin' to frighten you from recognisin' th' same fear that is in your own heart!

CLITHEROE (*struggling to release himself from* NORA). Damn you, woman, will you let me go!

CAPT. BRENNAN (*fiercely, to* CLITHEROE). Why are you beggin' her to let you go? Are you afraid of her, or what? Break her hold on you, man, or go up, an' sit on her lap!

(CLITHEROE *trying roughly to break her hold.*)

NORA (*imploringly*). Oh, Jack. . . . Jack. . . . Jack!

LIEUT. LANGON (*agonisingly*). Brennan, a priest; I'm dyin', I think, I'm dyin'!

CLITHEROE (*to* NORA). If you won't do it
quietly, I'll have to make you! (*To* BRENNAN)
Here, hold this gun, you, for a minute.

(*He hands the gun to* BRENNAN.)·

NORA (*pitifully*). Please, Jack. . . . You're
hurting me, Jack. . . . Honestly. . . . Oh,
you're hurting . . . me! . . . I won't, I
won't, I won't! . . . Oh, Jack, I gave you
everything you asked of me. . . . Don't fling
me from you, now!

(*He roughly loosens her grip, and pushes
her away from him,* NORA *sinks to the
ground and lies there.*)

NORA (*weakly*). Ah, Jack. . . . Jack. . . .
Jack!

CLITHEROE (*taking the gun back from* BRENNAN).
Come on, come on.

(*They go out.* BESSIE *looks at* NORA *lying
on the street, for a few moments, then,
leaving the window, she comes out, runs
over to* NORA, *lifts her up in her arms,
and carries her swiftly into the house.
A short pause, then down the street is
heard a wild, drunken yell; it comes
nearer, and* FLUTHER *enters, frenzied,
wild-eyed, mad, roaring drunk. In
his arms is an earthen half-gallon jar
of whisky; streaming from one of the*

*pockets of his coat is the arm of a new
tunic shirt; on his head is a woman's
vivid blue hat with gold lacing, all of
which he has looted.*)

FLUTHER (*singing in a frenzy*):

Fluther's a jolly good fella! . . . Fluther's a jolly
good fella!
Up th' rebels! .   . That nobody can deny!

(*He beats on the door.*)

Get us a mug or a jug, or somethin', some o'
yous, one o' yous, will yous, before I lay one
o' yous out! . . . (*Looking down the street*)
Bang an' fire away for all Fluther cares. . . .
(*Banging at door*) Come down an' open th'
door, some of yous, one o' yous, will yous,
before I lay some o' yous out! . . . Th' whole
city can topple home to hell, for Fluther!

(*Inside the house is heard a scream from
NORA followed by a moan.*)

FLUTHER (*singing furiously*):

That nobody can deny, that nobody can deny,
For Fluther's a jolly good fella, Fluther's a jolly good fella,
Fluther's a jolly good fella . . . Up th' rebels! That
nobody can deny!

(*His frantic movements cause him to spill
some of the whisky out of the jar.*)

Blast you, Fluther, don't be spillin' th'
precious liquor! (*He kicks at the door.*)   Ay,

give us a mug or a jug, or somethin', one o'
yous, some o' yous, will yous, before I lay one
o' yous out!

> (*The door suddenly opens, and* BESSIE,
> *coming out, grips him by the collar.*)

BESSIE (*indignantly*). You bowsey, come in
ower o' that. . . . I'll thrim your thricks o'
dhrunken dancin' for you, an' none of us
knowin' how soon we'll bump into a world
we were never in before!

FLUTHER (*as she is pulling him in*). Ay, th'
jar, th' jar, th' jar!

> (*A short pause, then again is heard a
> scream of pain from* NORA. *The door
> opens and* MRS. GOGAN *and* BESSIE *are
> seen standing at it.*)

BESSIE. Fluther would go, only he's too
dhrunk, . . . Oh, God, isn't it a pity he's so
dhrunk! We'll have to thry to get a docthor
somewhere.

MRS. GOGAN. I'd be afraid to go. . . . Besides, Mollser's terrible bad. I don't think
you'll get a docthor to come. It's hardly any
use goin'.

BESSIE (*determinedly*). I'll risk it. . . . Give
her a little of Fluther's whisky. . . . It's th'
fright that's brought it on her so soon. . . .
Go on back to her, you.

(MRS. GOGAN *goes in, and* BESSIE *softly closes the door. She is moving forward, when the sound of some rifle shots, and the tok, tok, tok of a distant machine-gun bring her to a sudden halt. She hesitates for a moment, then she tightens her shawl round her, as if it were a shield, then she firmly and swiftly goes out.*)

BESSIE (*as she goes out*). Oh, God, be Thou my help in time o' throuble. An' shelter me safely in th' shadow of Thy wings!

CURTAIN

ACT IV

(The living-room of BESSIE BURGESS. *It is one of
two small attic rooms (the other, used as a
bedroom, is to the Left), the ceiling slopes up
towards the back, giving to the apartment a
look of compressed confinement. In the centre
of the ceiling is a small skylight. There is an
unmistakable air of poverty bordering on
destitution. The paper on the walls is torn
and soiled, particularly near the fire where the
cooking is done, and near the washstand,
where the washing is done. The fireplace
is to the Left. A small armchair near fire.
Two small windows at Back. A pane of one
of these windows is starred by the entrance of
a bullet. Under the window to the Right is
an oak coffin standing on two kitchen chairs.
Near the coffin is a home-manufactured stool,
on which are two lighted candles. Between
the two windows is a worn-out dresser on
which is a small quantity of delph. Tattered
remains of cheap lace curtains drape the*

windows. Standing near the window on Left is a brass standing-lamp with a fancy shade; hanging on the wall near the same window is a vividly crimson silk dress, both of which have been looted. A door on Left leading to the bedroom. Another opposite giving a way to the rest of the house. To the Left of this door a common washstand. A tin kettle, very black, and an old saucepan inside the fender. There is no light in the room but that given from the two candles and the fire. The dusk has well fallen, and the glare of the burning buildings in the town can be seen through the windows in the distant sky. The COVEY *and* FLUTHER *have been playing cards, sitting on the floor by the light of the candles on the stool near the coffin. When the curtain rises the* COVEY *is shuffling the cards,* PETER *is sitting in a stiff, dignified way beside him, and* FLUTHER *is kneeling beside the window Left, cautiously looking out. It is a few days later.)*

FLUTHER (*furtively peeping out of the window*). Give them a good shuffling. . . . Th' sky's gettin' reddher an' reddher. . . . You'd think it was afire. . . . Half o' th' city must be burnin'.

THE COVEY. If I was you, Fluther, I'd keep away from that window. . . . It's dangerous, an', besides, if they see you, you'll only bring a nose on th' house.

PETER. Yes; an' he knows we had to leave our own place th' way they were riddlin' it with machine-gun fire. . . . He'll keep on pimpin' an' pimpin' there, till we have to fly out o' this place too.

FLUTHER (*ironically*). If they make any attack here, we'll send you out in your green an' glory uniform, shakin' your sword over your head, an' they'll fly before you as th' Danes flew before Brian Boru!

THE COVEY (*placing the cards on the floor, after shuffling them*). Come on, an' cut.

    (FLUTHER *comes over, sits on floor, and cuts the cards.*)

THE COVEY (*having dealt the cards*). Spuds up again.

    (NORA *moans feebly in room on Left.*)

FLUTHER. There, she's at it again. She's been quiet for a good long time, all th' same.

THE COVEY. She was quiet before, sure, an' she broke out again worse than ever. . . . What was led that time?

PETER. Thray o' Hearts, Thray o' Hearts, Thray o' Hearts.

FLUTHER. It's damned hard lines to think of her dead-born kiddie lyin' there in th' arms o' poor little Mollser. Mollser snuffed it, sudden too, afther all.

THE COVEY. Sure she never got any care. How could she get it, an' th' mother out day an' night lookin' for work, an' her consumptive husband leavin' her with a baby to be born before he died.

VOICES IN A LILTING CHANT TO THE LEFT IN A DISTANT STREET. Red Cr . . . oss, Red Cr . . . oss! . . . Ambu . . . lance, Ambu . . . lance!

THE COVEY (*to* FLUTHER). Your deal, Fluther.

FLUTHER (*shuffling and dealing the cards*). It'll take a lot out o' Nora—if she'll ever be th' same.

THE COVEY. Th' docthor thinks she'll never be th' same; thinks she'll be a little touched here. (*He touches his forehead.*) She's ramblin' a lot; thinkin' she's out in th' counthry with Jack; or, gettin' his dinner ready for him before he comes home; or, yellin' for her kiddie. All that, though, might be th' chloroform she got. . . . I don't know what we'd have done only for oul' Bessie: up with her for th' past three nights, hand runnin'.

FLUTHER. I always knew there was never

anything really derogatory wrong with poor, oul' Bessie. (*To* PETER *who is taking a trick*) Ay, houl' on, there, don't be so damn quick— that's my thrick.

PETER. What's your thrick?   It's my thrick, man.

FLUTHER (*loudly*). How is it your thrick?

PETER (*answering as loudly*). Didn't I lead th' deuce!

FLUTHER. You must be gettin' blind, man; don't you see th' ace?

BESSIE (*appearing at door of room, Left; in a tense whisper*).   D'ye want to waken her again on me, when she's just gone asleep?   If she wakes will yous come an' mind her?   If I hear a whisper out o' one o' yous again, I'll . . . gut yous!

THE COVEY (*in a whisper*). S-s-s-h. She can hear anything above a whisper.

PETER (*looking up at the ceiling*). Th' gentle an' merciful God 'll give th' pair o' yous a scawldin' an' a scarifyin' one o' these days!

> (FLUTHER *takes a bottle of whisky from his pocket, and takes a drink.*)

THE COVEY (*to* FLUTHER). Why don't you spread that out, man, an' thry to keep a sup for to-morrow?

FLUTHER. Spread it out?   Keep a sup for

to-morrow? How th' hell does a fella know there'll be any to-morrow? If I'm goin' to be whipped away, let me be whipped away when it's empty, an' not when it's half full! (*To* BESSIE, *who has seated herself in an armchair at the fire*) How is she, now, Bessie?

BESSIE. I left her sleeping quietly. When I'm listenin' to her babblin', I think she'll never be much betther than she is. Her eyes have a hauntin' way of lookin' in instead of lookin' out, as if her mind had been lost alive in madly minglin' memories of th' past. . . . (*Sleepily*) Crushin' her thoughts . . . together . . . in a fierce . . . an' fanciful . . . (*she nods her head and starts wakefully*) idea that dead things are livin', an' livin' things are dead. . . . (*With a start*) Was that a scream I heard her give? (*Reassured*) Blessed God, I think I hear her screamin' every minute! An' it's only there with me that I'm able to keep awake.

THE COVEY. She'll sleep, maybe, for a long time, now. Ten there.

FLUTHER. Ten here. If she gets a long sleep, she might be all right. Peter's th' lone five.

THE COVEY. Whisht! I think I hear somebody movin' below. Whoever it is, he's comin' up.

(*A pause. Then the door opens and* CAPTAIN BRENNAN *comes into the room. He has changed his uniform for a suit of civies. His eyes droop with the heaviness of exhaustion; his face is pallid and drawn. His clothes are dusty and stained here and there with mud. He leans heavily on the back of a chair as he stands.*)

CAPT. BRENNAN. Mrs. Clitheroe; where's Mrs. Clitheroe? I was told I'd find her here.

BESSIE. What d'ye want with Mrs. Clitheroe?

CAPT. BRENNAN. I've a message, a last message for her from her husband.

BESSIE. Killed! He's not killed, is he!

CAPT. BRENNAN (*sinking stiffly and painfully on to a chair*). In th' Imperial Hotel; we fought till th' place was in flames. He was shot through th' arm, an' then through th' lung. . . . I could do nothin' for him—only watch his breath comin' an' goin' in quick, jerky gasps, an' a tiny sthream o' blood thricklin' out of his mouth, down over his lower lip. . . . I said a prayer for th' dyin', an' twined his Rosary beads around his fingers. . . . Then I had to leave him to save meself. . . . (*He shows some holes in his coat*) Look at th' way a machine-gun tore at me coat, as I belted out o' th' buildin' an' darted across th' sthreet for shelter. . . .

113   I

An' then, I seen The Plough an' th' Stars fallin' like a shot as th' roof crashed in, an' where I'd left poor Jack was nothin' but a leppin' spout o' flame!

BESSIE (*with partly repressed vehemence*). Ay, you left him! You twined his Rosary beads round his fingers, an' then, you run like a hare to get out o' danger!

CAPT. BRENNAN. I took me chance as well as him. . . . He took it like a man. His last whisper was to " Tell Nora to be brave; that I'm ready to meet my God, an' that I'm proud to die for Ireland." An' when our General heard it he said that "Commandant Clitheroe's end was a gleam of glory." Mrs. Clitheroe's grief will be a joy when she realises that she has had a hero for a husband.

BESSIE. If you only seen her, you'd know to th' differ.

(NORA *appears at door, Left. She is clad only in her nightdress; her hair, uncared for some days, is hanging in disorder over her shoulders. Her pale face looks paler still because of a vivid red spot on the tip of each cheek. Her eyes are glimmering with the light of incipient insanity; her hands are nervously fiddling with her nightgown. She halts at the door for a moment, looks*

114

vacantly around the room, and then comes slowly in.   The rest do not notice her till she speaks.)

NORA (*in a quiet and monotonous tone*). No . . . Not there, Jack. . . . I can feel comfortable only in our own familiar place beneath th' bramble tree. . . . We must be walking for a long time; I feel very, very tired. . . . Have we to go farther, or have we passed it by? (*Passing her hand across her eyes*) Curious mist on my eyes. . . . Why don't you hold my hand, Jack. . . . (*Excitedly*) No, no, Jack, it's not. Can't you see it's a goldfinch. Look at th' black-satiny wings with th' gold bars, an' th' splash of crimson on its head. . . . (*Wearily*) Something ails me, something ails me. . . . Don't kiss me like that; you take my breath away, Jack. . . . Why do you frown at me? . . . You're going away, and (*frightened*) I can't follow you! Something's keeping me from moving. . . . (*Crying out*) Jack, Jack, Jack!

BESSIE (*who has gone over and caught* NORA's *arm*). Now, Mrs. Clitheroe, you're a terrible woman to get up out of bed. . . . You'll get cold if you stay here in them clothes.

NORA. Cold? I'm feelin' very cold; it's chilly out here in th' counthry. . . . (*Looking around, frightened*) What place is this? Where am I?

BESSIE (*coaxingly*). You're all right, Nora; you're with friends, an' in a safe place. Don't you know your uncle an' your cousin, an' poor oul' Fluther?

PETER (*about to go over to* NORA). Nora, darlin', now——

FLUTHER (*pulling him back*). Now, leave her to Bessie, man. A crowd 'll only make her worse.

NORA (*thoughtfully*). There is something I want to remember, an' I can't. (*With agony*) I can't, I can't, I can't! My head, my head! (*Suddenly breaking from* BESSIE, *and running over to the men, and gripping* FLUTHER *by the shoulders*) Where is it? Where's my baby? Tell me where you've put it, where've you hidden it? My baby, my baby; I want my baby! My head, my poor head. . . . Oh, I can't tell what is wrong with me. (*Screaming*) Give him to me, give me my husband!

BESSIE. Blessin' o' God on us, isn't this pitiful!

NORA (*struggling with* BESSIE). I won't go away for you; I won't. Not till you give me back my husband. (*Screaming*) Murderers, that's what yous are; murderers, murderers!

BESSIE. S-s-sh. We'll bring Mr. Clitheroe back to you, if you'll only lie down an' stop quiet. . . . (*Trying to lead her in*) Come on, now, Nora, an' I'll sing something to you.

NORA. I feel as if my life was thryin' to force its way out of my body. . . . I can hardly breathe . . . I'm frightened, I'm frightened, I'm frightened! For God's sake, don't leave me, Bessie. Hold my hand, put your arms around me!

FLUTHER (*to* BRENNAN). Now you can see th' way she is, man.

PETER. An' what way would she be if she heard Jack had gone west?

THE COVEY (*to* PETER). Shut up, you, man!

BESSIE (*to* NORA). We'll have to be brave, an' let patience clip away th' heaviness of th' slow-movin' hours, rememberin' that sorrow may endure for th' night, but joy cometh in th' mornin'. . . . Come on in, an' I'll sing to you, an' you'll rest quietly.

NORA (*stopping suddenly on her way to the room*). Jack an' me are goin' out somewhere this evenin'. Where I can't tell. Isn't it curious I can't remember. . . . Maura, Maura, Jack, if th' baby's a girl; any name you like, if th' baby's a boy! . . . He's there. (*Scream-*

ing) He's there, an' they won't give him back to me!

BESSIE. S-ss-s-h, darlin', s-ssh. I won't sing to you, if you're not quiet.

NORA (*nervously holding* BESSIE). Hold my hand, hold my hand, an' sing to me, sing to me!

BESSIE. Come in an' lie down, an' I'll sing to you.

NORA (*vehemently*). Sing to me, sing to me; sing, sing!

BESSIE (*singing as she leads* NORA *into room*):

Lead, kindly light, amid th' encircling gloom,
  Lead Thou me on.
Th' night is dark an' I am far from home,
  Lead Thou me on.
Keep Thou my feet, I do not ask to see
Th' distant scene—one step enough for me.

So long that Thou hast blessed me, sure Thou still
  Will lead me on;

      (*They go in.*)

BESSIE (*singing in room*):

O'er moor an' fen, o'er crag an' torrent, till
  Th' night is gone.
An' in th' morn those angel faces smile
That I have lov'd long since, an' lost awhile!

THE COVEY (*to* BRENNAN). Now that you've seen how bad she is, an' that we daren't tell her what has happened till she's betther, you'd best be slippin' back to where you come from.

CAPT. BRENNAN. There's no chance o' slippin' back now, for th' military are everywhere: a fly couldn't get through.   I'd never have got here, only I managed to change me uniform for what I'm wearin'. . . . I'll have to take me chance, an' thry to lie low here for a while.

THE COVEY (*frightened*). There's no place here to lie low.   Th' Tommies 'll be hoppin' in here, any minute!

PETER (*aghast*). An' then we'd all be shanghaied!

THE COVEY. Be God, there's enough afther happenin' to us!

FLUTHER (*warningly, as he listens*). Whisht, whisht, th' whole o' yous.   I think I heard th' clang of a rifle butt on th' floor of th' hall below. (*All alertness*) Here, come on with th' cards again.   I'll deal.

(*He shuffles and deals the cards to all.*)

FLUTHER. Clubs up. (*To* BRENNAN) Thry to keep your hands from shakin' man.   You lead, Peter. (*As* PETER *throws out a card*) Four o' Hearts led.

(*The door opens and* CORPORAL STODDART *of the Wiltshires enters in full war kit;*

steel helmet, rifle and bayonet and
trench tools. He looks round the room.
A pause and a palpable silence.)

FLUTHER (*breaking the silence*). Two tens an'
a five.

CORPORAL STODDART. 'ello. (*Indicating the*
coffin) This the stiff?

THE COVEY. Yis.

CORPORAL STODDART. Who's gowing with it?
Ownly one allowed to gow with it, you knaow.

THE COVEY. I dunno.

CORPORAL STODDART. You dunnow?

THE COVEY. I dunno.

BESSIE (*coming into the room*). She's afther
slippin' off to sleep again, thanks be to God.
I'm hardly able to keep me own eyes open.
(*To the soldier*) Oh, are yous goin' to take away
poor little Mollser?

CORPORAL STODDART. Ay; 'oo's agowing
with 'er?

BESSIE. Oh, th' poor mother, o' course.
God help her, it's a terrible blow to her!

FLUTHER. A terrible blow? Sure, she's in
her element now, woman, mixin' earth to earth,
an' ashes t'ashes an' dust to dust, an' revellin'
in plumes an' hearses, last days an' judgements!

BESSIE (*falling into chair by the fire*). God
bless us! I'm jaded!

CORPORAL STODDART. Was she plugged?

THE COVEY. Ah, no; died o' consumption.

CORPORAL STODDART. How, is that hall? Thought she moight 'ave been plugged.

THE COVEY. Is that all? Isn't it enough? D'ye know, comrade, that more die o' consumption than are killed in th' wars? An' it's all because of th' system we're livin' undher?

CORPORAL STODDART. Ow, Oi knaow. Oi'm a Sowcialist moiself, but Oi 'as to do moi dooty.

THE COVEY (*ironically*). Dooty! Th' only dooty of a Socialist is th' emancipation of th' workers.

CORPORAL STODDART. Ow, a man's a man, an 'e 'as to foight for 'is country, 'asn't 'e?

FLUTHER (*aggressively*). You're not fightin' for your counthry here, are you?

PETER (*anxiously, to* FLUTHER). Ay, ay, Fluther, none o' that, none o' that!

THE COVEY. Fight for your counthry! Did y'ever read, comrade, Jenersky's *Thesis on the Origin, Development an' Consolidation of th' Evolutionary Idea of the Prolitariat*?

CORPORAL STODDART. Ow, cheese it, Paddy, cheese it!

BESSIE (*sleepily*). How is things in th' town, Tommy?

CORPORAL STODDART. Ow, Hoi fink hit's nearly howver. We've got 'em surrounded,

hand we're clowsing hin hon the bloighters.
Ow, hit was honly ha little bit hof ha dawg foight.

> (*The sharp ping of the sniper's rifle is
> heard, followed by a squeal of pain.*)

VOICES TO THE LEFT IN A CHANT. Red
Cr . . . oss, Red Cr . . . oss! Ambu . . .
lance, Ambu . . . lance!

CORPORAL STODDART (*excitedly*). Chroist, that's
hanother hof hour men 'it by that blawsted
snoiper! 'e's knocking abaht 'ere, some-
wheres. Gawd, when we gets th' bloighter,
we'll give 'im the cold steel, we will. We'll
jab the belly haht hof 'im, we will!

> (MRS. GOGAN *comes in tearfully, and a
> little proud of the importance of being
> directly connected with death.*)

MRS. GOGAN (*to* FLUTHER). I'll never forget
what you done for me, Fluther, goin' around
at th' risk of your life settlin' everything with
th' undhertaker an' th' cemetery people. When
all me own were afraid to put their noses out,
you plunged like a good one through hummin'
bullets, an' they knockin' fire out o' th' road,
tinklin' through th' frightened windows, an'
splashin' themselves to pieces on th' walls!
An' you'll find, that Mollser in th' happy place
she's gone to, won't forget to whisper, now an'
again, th' name o' Fluther.

CORPORAL STODDART. Git it aht, mother, git it aht.

BESSIE (*from the chair*). It's excusin' me you'll be, Mrs. Gogan, for not stannin' up, seein' I'm shaky on me feet for want of a little sleep, an' not desirin' to show any disrespect to poor little Mollser.

FLUTHER. Sure, we all know, Bessie, that it's vice versa with you.

MRS. GOGAN (*to* BESSIE). Indeed, it's meself that has well chronicled, Mrs. Burgess, all your gentle hurryin's to me little Mollser, when she was alive, bringin' her somethin' to dhrink, or somethin' t'eat, an' never passin' her without lifting up her heart with a delicate word o' kindness.

CORPORAL STODDART (*impatiently, but kindly*). Git it aht, git it aht, mother.

(*The* COVEY, FLUTHER, BRENNAN *and* PETER *carry out the coffin, followed by* MRS. GOGAN.)

CORPORAL STODDART (*to* BESSIE, *who is almost asleep*). 'Ow many men is in this 'ere 'ouse? (*No answer. Loudly*) 'Ow many men is in this 'ere 'ouse?

BESSIE (*waking with a start*). God, I was nearly asleep! . . . How many men? Didn't you see them?

123

CORPORAL STODDART. Are they hall that are hin the 'ouse?

BESSIE. Oh, there's none higher up, but there may be more lower down. Why?

CORPORAL STODDART. All men in the district 'as to be rounded up. Somebody's giving 'elp to the snoipers, hand we 'as to take precautions. If Oi 'ad my woy, Oi'd make 'em all join hup, hand do their bit! But Oi suppowse they hand you are all Shinners.

BESSIE (*who has been sinking into sleep, waking up to a sleepy vehemence*). Bessie Burgess is no Shinner, an' never had no thruck with anything spotted be th' fingers o' th' Fenians. But always made it her business to harness herself for Church whenever she knew that God Save The King was goin' to be sung at t'end of th' service; whose only son went to th' front in th' first contingent of the Dublin Fusiliers, an' that's on his way home carryin' a shatthered arm that he got fightin' for his King an' counthry!

> (*Her head sinks slowly forward again.*
> PETER *comes in to the room; his body
> is stiffened and his face is wearing a
> comically indignant look. He walks to
> and fro at the back of the room, evi-
> dently repressing a violent desire to speak*

angrily.   He is followed in by FLUTHER,
the COVEY *and* BRENNAN, *who slinks
into an obscure corner of the room,
nervous of notice.*)

FLUTHER (*after an embarrassing pause*). Th'
air in th' sthreet outside's shakin' with the firin'
o' rifles, an' machine-guns.   It must be a hot
shop in th' middle o' th' scrap.

CORPORAL STODDART. We're pumping lead
in on 'em from every side, now;   they'll soon
be shoving up th' white flag.

PETER (*with a shout*). I'm tellin' you either
o' yous two lowsers 'ud make a betther hearseman than Peter!   proddin' an' pokin' at me an'
I helpin' to carry out a corpse!

FLUTHER. It wasn't a very derogatory thing
for th' Covey to say that you'd make a fancy
hearseman, was it?

PETER (*furiously*). A pair o' redjesthered
bowseys pondherin' from mornin' till night
on how they'll get a chance to break a gap
through th' quiet nature of a man that's always
endeavourin' to chase out of him any sthray
thought of venom against his fella-man!

THE COVEY. Oh, shut it, shut it, shut it!

PETER. As long as I'm a livin' man, re-
sponsible for me thoughts, words an' deeds to
th' Man above, I'll feel meself instituted to

fight again' th' sliddherin' ways of a pair o' picaroons, whisperin', concurrin', concoctin', an' conspirin' together to rendher me unconscious of th' life I'm thryin' to live!

CORPORAL STODDART (*dumbfounded*). What's wrong, Daddy; wot 'ave they done to you?

PETER (*savagely to the Corporal*). You mind your own business! What's it got to do with you, what's wrong with me?

BESSIE (*in a sleepy murmur*). Will yous thry to conthrol yourselves into quietness? Yous'll waken her . . . up . . . on . . . me . . . again.

(*She sleeps.*)

FLUTHER. Come on, boys, to th' cards again, an' never mind him.

CORPORAL STODDART. Now use of you gowing to start cawds; you'll be gowing out hof 'ere, soon as Sergeant comes.

FLUTHER. Goin' out o' here? An' why'r we goin' out o' here?

CORPORAL STODDART. All men hin district to be rounded up, and 'eld hin till the scrap his hover.

FLUTHER. An' where'r we goin' to be held in?

CORPORAL STODDART. They're putting 'em in ha church.

THE COVEY. A church?

126

FLUTHER. What sort of a church? Is it a Protestan' Church?

CORPORAL STODDART. I dunnow; I suppowse so.

FLUTHER (*dismayed*). Be God, it'll be a nice thing to be stuck all night in a Protestan' Church!

CORPORAL STODDART. Bring the cawds; you moight get a chance of ha goime.

FLUTHER. Ah, no, that wouldn't do. . . . I wondher? (*After a moment's thought*) Ah, I don't think we'd be doin' anything derogatory be playin' cards in a Protestan' Church.

CORPORAL STODDART. If Oi was you Oi'd bring a little snack with me; you moight be glad of hit before the mawning. (*Sings*):

> Oi do loike a snoice mince poy,
> Oi do loike a snoice mince poy!

(*The snap of the sniper's rifle rings out again, followed simultaneously by a scream of pain.* CORPORAL STODDART *goes pale, and brings his rifle to the ready, listening.*)

VOICES CHANTING TO THE RIGHT. Red Cro . . . ss, Red Cro . . . ss! Ambu . . . lance, Ambu . . . lance!

(SERGEANT TINLEY *comes rapidly in, pale, agitated, and fiercely angry.*)

CORPORAL STODDART (*to* SERGEANT). One of hour men 'it, Sargeant?

SERGEANT TINLEY. Private Taylor; got 'it roight through the chest, 'e did; han 'owl in front hof 'im has 'ow you could put your fist through, hand arf 'e's back blown awoy! Dum dum bullets they're using. Gang hof Hassassins potting at hus from behind roofs. That's not ploying the goime: why down't they come hinto the howpen hand foight fair!

FLUTHER (*unable to stand the slight*). Fight fair! A few hundhred scrawls o' chaps with a couple o' guns an' Rosary beads, again' a hundhred thousand thrained men with horse, fut an' artillery . . . an' he wants us to fight fair! (*To* SARGEANT) D'ye want us to come out in our skins an' throw stones?

SERGEANT TINLEY (*to* CORPORAL). Are these four all that are 'ere?

CORPORAL STODDART. Four; that's hall, Sargeant.

SERGEANT TINLEY (*vindictively*). Come on, then; get the bloighters aht. (*To the men*) 'Ere, 'op hit aht! Aht hinto the streets with you, and if a snoiper sends hanother of hour men west, you gow with 'im! (*He catches* FLUTHER *by the shoulder*) Gow hon, git aht!

128

FLUTHER. Eh, who are you chuckin', eh?

SERGEANT TINLEY (*roughly*). Gow hon, git aht, you bloighter.

FLUTHER. Who are you callin' a bloighter to, eh? I'm a Dublin man, born an' bred in th' city, see?

SERGEANT TINLEY. Oi down't care if you were Broin Buroo; git aht, git aht.

FLUTHER (*halting as he is going out*). Jasus, you an' your guns! Leave them down, an' I'd beat th' two o' yous without sweatin'!

(PETER, BRENNAN, *the* COVEY and FLUTHER, *followed by the soldiers, go out.* BESSIE *is sleeping heavily on the chair by the fire. After a pause,* NORA *appears at door, Left, in her night-dress. Remaining at door for a few moments she looks vaguely around the room. She then comes in quietly, goes over to the fire, pokes it and puts the kettle on. She thinks for a few moments, pressing her hand to her forehead. She looks questioningly at the fire, and then at the press at back. She goes to the press, opens it, takes out a soiled cloth and spreads it on the table. She then places things for tea on the table.*)

NORA. I imagine th' room looks very odd,

somehow. . . . I was nearly forgetting Jack's
tea. . . . Ah, I think I'll have everything done
before he gets in. . . . (*She lilts gently, as she
arranges the table.*)

> Th' violets were scenting th' woods, Nora,
>   Displaying their charms to th' bee,
> When I first said I lov'd only you, Nora,
>   An' you said you lov'd only me.

> Th' chestnut blooms gleam'd through th'glade, Nora,
>   A robin sang loud from a tree,
> When I first said I lov'd only you, Nora,
>   An' you said you loved only me.

> (*She pauses suddenly, and glances round
>   the room.*)

NORA (*doubtfully*). I can't help feelin' this
room very strange. . . . What is it? . . .
What is it? . . . I must think. . . . I must
thry to remember. . . .

VOICES CHANTING IN A DISTANT STREET.
Ambu . . . lance, Ambu . . . lance! Red
Cro . . . ss, Red Cro . . . ss!

NORA (*startled and listening for a moment, then
resuming the arrangement of the table*).

> Trees, birds an' bees sang a song, Nora,
>   Of happier transports to be,
> When I first said I lov'd only you, Nora,
>   An' you said you lov'd only me.

130

(*A burst of rifle fire is heard in a street near by, followed by the rapid rok, tok, tok, of a machine-gun.*)

NORA (*staring in front of her and screaming*). Jack, Jack, Jack! My baby, my baby, my baby!

BESSIE (*waking with a start*). You divil, are you afther gettin' out o' bed again!

(*She rises and runs towards* NORA, *who rushes to the window, which she frantically opens.*)

NORA (*at window, screaming*). Jack, Jack, for God's sake, come to me!

SOLDIERS (*outside, shouting*). Git awoy, git awoy from that window, there!

BESSIE (*seizing hold of* NORA). Come away, come away, woman, from that window!

NORA (*struggling with* BESSIE). Where is it; where have you hidden it? Oh, Jack, Jack, where are you?

BESSIE (*imploringly*). Mrs. Clitheroe, for God's sake, come away!

NORA (*fiercely*). I won't; he's below. Let . . . me . . . go! You're thryin' to keep me from me husband. I'll follow him. Jack, Jack, come to your Nora!

BESSIE. Hus-s-sh, Nora, Nora! He'll be here in a minute. I'll bring him to you,

131

if you'll only be quiet—honest to God, I will.

> (*With a great effort* BESSIE *pushes* NORA
> *away from the window, the force used
> causing her to stagger against it herself.
> Two rifle shots ring out in quick succes-
> sion.* BESSIE *jerks her body convulsively;
> stands stiffly upright for a moment, a
> look of agonized astonishment on her
> face, then she staggers forward, leaning
> heavily on the table with her hands.*)

BESSIE (*with an arrested scream of fear and
pain*). Merciful God, I'm shot, I'm shot, I'm
shot! . . . Th' life's pourin' out o' me! (*To*
NORA) I've got this through . . . through
you . . . through you, you bitch, you! . . .
O God, have mercy on me! . . . (*To* NORA)
You wouldn't stop quiet, no you wouldn't, you
wouldn't, blast you! Look at what I'm afther
gettin', look at what I'm afther gettin' . . .
I'm bleedin' to death, an' no one's here to stop
th' flowin' blood! (*Calling*) Mrs. Gogan, Mrs.
Gogan! Fluther, Fluther, for God's sake,
somebody, a doctor, a doctor!

> (*She staggers frightened towards the door,
> to seek for aid, but, weakening half-way
> across the room, she sinks to her knees,
> and bending forward, supports herself*

132

with her hands resting on the floor.
NORA *is standing rigidly with her back
to the wall opposite, her trembling hands
held out a little from the sides of her
body, her lips quivering, her breast
heaving, staring wildly at the figure of*
BESSIE.)

NORA (*in a breathless whisper*). Jack, I'm
frightened. . . . I'm frightened, Jack. . . .
Oh, Jack, where are you?

BESSIE (*moaningly*). This is what's afther
comin' on me for nursin' you day an' night.
. . . I was a fool, a fool, a fool! Get me a
dhrink o' wather, you jade, will you? There's
a fire burnin' in me blood! (*Pleadingly*) Nora,
Nora, dear, for God's sake, run out an' get
Mrs. Gogan, or Fluther, or somebody to bring
a doctor, quick, quick, quick! (*As* NORA *does
not stir*) Blast you, stir yourself, before I'm
gone!

NORA. Oh, Jack, Jack, where are you?

BESSIE (*in a whispered moan*). Jesus Christ,
me sight's goin'! It's all dark, dark! Nora,
hold me hand!

(BESSIE'S *body lists over and she sinks into
a prostrate position on the floor.*)

BESSIE. I'm dyin', I'm dyin' . . . I feel
it. . . . Oh God, oh God! (*She feebly sings*)

133

I do believe, I will believe
    That Jesus died for me;
That on th' cross He shed His blood,
    From sin to set me free. . . .

I do believe . . . I will believe
    . . . Jesus died . . . me;
. . . th' cross He shed . . . blood,
    From sin . . . free.

(*She ceases singing, and lies stretched out,
still and very rigid. A pause. Then*
MRS. GOGAN *runs hastily in.*)

MRS. GOGAN (*quivering with fright*). Blessed
be God, what's afther happenin'? (*To* NORA)
What's wrong, child, what's wrong? (*She
sees* BESSIE, *runs to her and bends over the body*)
Bessie, Bessie! (*She shakes the body*) Mrs.
Burgess, Mrs. Burgess! (*She feels* BESSIE's
forehead) My God, she's as cold as death.
They're afther murdherin' th' poor inoffensive
woman!

(SERGEANT TINLEY *and* CORPORAL
STODDART *enter agitatedly, their rifles
at the ready.*)

SERGEANT TINLEY (*excitedly*). This is the 'ouse.
That's the window!

NORA (*pressing back against the wall*). Hide
it, hide it; cover it up, cover it up!

SERGEANT TINLEY (*going over to the body*). 'Ere,

what's this? Who's this? (*Looking at* BESSIE) Ow Gawd, we've plugged one of the women of the 'ouse.

CORPORAL STODDART. Whoy the 'ell did she gow to the window? Is she dead?

SERGEANT TINLEY. Ow, dead as bedamned. Well, we couldn't afford to toike any chawnces.

NORA (*screaming*). Hide it, hide it; don't let me see it! Take me away, take me away, Mrs. Gogan!

> (MRS. GOGAN *runs into room, Left, and runs out again with a sheet which she spreads over the body of* BESSIE.)

MRS. GOGAN (*as she spreads the sheet*). Oh, God help her, th' poor woman, she's stiffenin' out as hard as she can! Her face has written on it th' shock o' sudden agony, an' her hands is whitenin' into th' smooth shininess of wax.

NORA (*whimperingly*). Take me away, take me away; don't leave me here to be lookin' an' lookin' at it!

MRS. GOGAN (*going over to* NORA *and putting her arm around her*). Come on with me, dear, an' you can doss in poor Mollser's bed, till we gather some neighbours to come an' give th' last friendly touches to Bessie in th' lonely layin' of her out.

> (MRS. GOGAN *and* NORA *go slowly out.*)

CORPORAL STODDART (*who has been looking around*, *to* SERGEANT TINLEY). Tea here, Sergeant. Wot abaht a cup of scald?

SERGEANT TINLEY. Pour it hout, Stoddart, pour it hout. Oi could scoff hanything just naow.

> (CORPORAL STODDART *pours out two cups of tea, and the two soldiers begin to drink. In the distance is heard a bitter burst of rifle and machine-gun fire, interspersed with the boom, boom of artillery. The glare in the sky seen through the window flares into a fuller and a deeper red.*)

SERGEANT TINLEY. There gows the general attack on the Powst Office.

VOICES IN A DISTANT STREET. Ambu . . . lance, Ambu . . . lance! Red Cro . . . ss, Red Cro . . . ss!

> (*The voices of soldiers at a barricade outside the house are heard singing.*)

They were summoned from the 'illside,
They were called in from the glen,
And the country found 'em ready
At the stirring call for men.
Let not tears add to their 'ardship,
As the soldiers pass along,
And although our 'eart is breaking,
Make it sing this cheery song.

WORKS BY JAMES STEPHENS

POETRY

A POETRY RECITAL. Crown 8vo. 3s. 6d. net.
GREEN BRANCHES. Crown 8vo. 1s. net.
THE ADVENTURES OF SEUMAS BEG: THE ROCKY
    ROAD TO DUBLIN. Crown 8vo. 4s. 6d. net.
REINCARNATIONS. Crown 8vo. 3s. 6d. net.
THE HILL OF VISION. Crown 8vo. 6s. net.
SONGS FROM THE CLAY. Crown 8vo. 4s. 6d. net.

PROSE

THE CROCK OF GOLD. Crown 8vo. 6s. net.
THE CROCK OF GOLD. With 12 Illustrations in Colour,
    and Headings and Tail-pieces in Black and White, by
    THOMAS MACKENZIE. Medium 8vo.
        Also a *Large-Paper Edition* on hand-made paper,
    limited to 500 copies, and each copy signed by
    Mr. STEPHENS. Super royal 8vo. [*In the press.*
THE CROCK OF GOLD. With Illustrations in Colour
    and Black and White by WILFRED JONES. 8vo. 12s. net.
DEIRDRE. Crown 8vo. 7s. 6d. net.
IN THE LAND OF YOUTH. Crown 8vo. 7s. 6d. net.
HERE ARE LADIES. Crown 8vo. 6s. net.
THE DEMI-GODS. Crown 8vo. 6s. net.
THE CHARWOMAN'S DAUGHTER. Crown 8vo.
    4s. 6d. net.
IRISH FAIRY TALES. Crown 8vo. 7s. 6d. net.
IRISH FAIRY TALES. With Illustrations in Colour
    and in Black and White by ARTHUR RACKHAM.
    Medium 8vo. 10s. net.

MACMILLAN AND CO., LTD., LONDON.

BY SEAN O'CASEY

TWO PLAYS: JUNO AND THE PAYCOCK; THE SHADOW OF A GUNMAN.
Crown 8vo.   7s. 6d. net.

"We all know how moving 'Juno and the Paycock' and 'The Shadow of a Gunman' may be when acted superbly, as they were in Dublin. We did not ask ourselves whether this was literature, because it moved us as life itself. . . . Now the plays are printed, and reading without the advantage of superb acting to bias judgment, 'Juno and the Paycock' appears no less moving to the imagination than it was when performed. . . . I think, after reading 'Juno and the Paycock,' that it is one of the greatest of Irish plays."—A. E. in *The Irish Statesman*.

"The most remarkable of our new dramatists is Sean O'Casey. . . . He captures to perfection the life of the Dublin slums. . . . I have no hesitation in thinking Sean O'Casey to be the most remarkable dramatist the Irish theatre has had since Mr. T. C. Murray."—Mr. LENNOX ROBINSON in *The Observer*.

"They are the finest things of their kind that have come out of Ireland since Synge. . . . These plays have the touch of greatness. In no dramatic essential are they lacking."—Mr. C. E. LAWRENCE in *The Bookman*.

"Mr. Sean O'Casey is the Abbey Theatre's new dramatist, and in many ways, perhaps, the greatest dramatist whose work has been seen there. . . . Fun and terror can seldom have been so mingled before."
—*The Daily News*.

MACMILLAN AND CO., LTD., LONDON.

I

SERGEANT TINLEY *and* CORPORAL STODDART
(*joining in the chorus, as they sip the tea*).

> Keep the 'owme fires burning,
> While your 'earts are yearning;
> Though your lads are far away
> They dream of 'owme;
> There's a silver loining
> Through the dark cloud shoining,
> Turn the dark cloud inside out,
> Till the boys come 'owme!

CURTAIN

Printed in Great Britain by R. & R. CLARK, LIMITED, *Edinburgh.*

WORKS BY W. B. YEATS

THE COLLECTED WORKS

*Attractively bound in green cloth, with
cover design by CHARLES RICKETT*

Crown 8vo. 10s. 6d. net each

LATER POEMS.

PLAYS IN PROSE AND VERSE.

PLAYS AND CONTROVERSIES.

ESSAYS.

EARLY POEMS AND STORIES.

RESPONSIBILITIES AND OTHER POEMS. Crown
8vo. 6s. net.

THE WILD SWANS AT COOLE. Poems. Crown 8vo.
5s. net.

FOUR PLAYS FOR DANCERS. Illustrated by
EDMUND DULAC. Fcap 4to. 10s. 6d. net.

THE PLAYER QUEEN. Globe 8vo. 2s. net.

STORIES OF RED HANRAHAN, ETC. Crown 8vo.
6s. net.

REVERIES OVER CHILDHOOD AND YOUTH.
Illustrated. Crown 8vo. 6s. net.

THE CUTTING OF AN AGATE. Essays. Crown 8vo.
6s. net.

MACMILLAN AND CO., LTD., LONDON.

3

WORKS BY A. E.

POETRY

COLLECTED POEMS. Crown 8vo. 7s. 6d. net.
VOICES OF THE STONES. Crown 8vo. 3s. 6d. net.

PROSE

THE CANDLE OF VISION. Crown 8vo. 6s. net.
THE INTERPRETERS. Crown 8vo. 6s. net.
IMAGINATIONS AND REVERIES. Crown 8vo. 7s. 6d. net.
THE NATIONAL BEING: Some Thoughts on an Irish
    Polity. Crown 8vo. 5s. net.

WORKS BY PADRAIC COLUM

POETRY

DRAMATIC LEGENDS AND OTHER POEMS. Crown
    8vo. 7s. 6d. net.
WILD EARTH AND OTHER POEMS. Crown 8vo.
    3s. 6d. net.

PROSE

CASTLE CONQUER. A Novel. Crown 8vo. 3s. 6d. net.

A GOLDEN TREASURY OF IRISH VERSE. Edited by
    LENNOX ROBINSON. Crown 8vo. Cloth, 7s. 6d. net.
    Leather, 10s. net.
POEMS BY WILLIAM ALLINGHAM. Selected and
    Arranged by HELEN ALLINGHAM. Pott 8vo. 3s. 6d. net.
                                    [*Golden Treasury Series.*
THOMAS MOORE. By STEPHEN GWYNN. Crown 8vo.
    3s. 6d. net.   [*English Men of Letters.*

MACMILLAN AND CO., LTD., LONDON.

4